CRC
FAMILY
PORTRAIT

CRC FAMILY PORTRAIT
Sketches Of Ordinary Christians In A 125-Year-Old Church

James C. Schaap

Board of Publications of the Christian Reformed Church
Grand Rapids, Michigan

Library of Congress Cataloging in Publication Data

Schaap, James C., 1948-
  CRC family portrait.

   1. Christian Reformed Church—Biography.
I. Title.
BX6841.S3   1982   285.7'31'0922 [B]   82-22625
ISBN 0-933140-60-6

©1982 by the Board of Publications of the Christian Reformed Church
2850 Kalamazoo Ave. SE
Grand Rapids, Michigan 49560

Printed in the United States of America

Contents

Preface

More than anyone else, perhaps, the Nick Veldhuisen family of Emo, Ontario, is responsible for the idea of the *CRC Family Portrait.* In May 1980, I enjoyed the Veldhuisen hospitality, listened to their stories of bears and wolves, watched a calf being born in their barn, and ate breakfasts at their huge kitchen table. For three days I lived with them, and slowly the idea came to me that here in the Ontario wilderness was a CRC family that the rest of us should know. So I borrowed the oldest son's camera and took some homey shots in between the speeches I gave at the youth league retreat being hosted by the Emo church.

Five hundred miles south, back home again, I sat over the typewriter, trying to recreate the *gezelligheid,* the sights and sounds, of the Veldhuisen kitchen. And when the story was finished, something told me the Veldhuisens were only the beginning.

By July 1980, a series was arranged: the chapters in this book first appeared as articles in *The Banner,* the weekly magazine of the Christian Reformed Church, between September 1981 and August 1982. There were thirty stories in all (the number eventually grew), individual narratives about Christian Reformed people, members of a denomination soon to be reaching its 125th birthday.

The Schaap family was then living in Oostburg, Wisconsin, attending a church temporarily without what elders call an "undershepherd." Guest ministers became the first source of more possible subjects: from Rev. Gerry Heyboer, then of Delavan, Wisconsin, Grandma Los; from Madison, Wisconsin's Rev. Gerald Frens, Dr. Condon Vander Ark. By December, I learned not to trust the batteries in my K-Mart tape recorder; I missed nearly a half hour of Vander Ark's technical explanation of cardiology. When I got home, the taped conversation was little more than a chorus of horrid droning.

By the summer of 1981, when I did most of the traveling, I became more selective in choosing subjects, conscious of trying to maintain a consistent number of men and women, old and young, rich and poor, professional and blue-collar. At times I asked preachers for names; at times I called on old friends for help, old friends like Gerry Ebbers of Edmonton, Alberta, people I guessed would know the folks in their communities. Gerry gave me a long list of Edmonton residents; over the phone we talked about his suggestions until I felt sure I had found my subject.

Generally, the interviews themselves lasted three to four hours. On occasion I was able to spend more time with the people I interviewed—Bill Oostenbrink took me up into the foothills of the Canadian Rockies to see an exploratory oil rig; Boet Gilde arranged to have me ride shotgun on his all-night beat through the vacant streets of West Palm Beach, Florida. But mostly it was simple conversation: early Saturday morning breakfast at Edgerton's Leader Cafe or afternoon coffee at Marly Visser's farm. And mostly I asked just two questions: "Who are you?" and "What do you think about the church?" That two easy questions could push through four long hours never ceased to amaze me.

We can probably learn a number of things from the portraits; we Calvinists like to moralize. Historians, theologians, sociologists, even psychologists may all have their chance. But as a writer I learned simply that everyone has a story. Some of our stories are joyous, some are tragic; some rollicking, some miraculous. Some are exotic, some typical; some are pathetic, and some especially blessed. But always there was a story —and I'd leave a front porch or a kitchen table or a front-room rocker thinking how easy it is to be a writer. All we need to do is listen.

To my family for their gift of time, to *Banner* editor Andrew Kuyvenhoven and A. James Heynen for their gift of trust, to the folks herein for their gifts of themselves, and to our God for his gifts of grace—to all of these I owe my thanks.

And finally I wish to thank those who helped me by supplying names or offering their warm hospitality: Mr. Howard Bielema, Chicago; Morris Blankespoor, Pella, Iowa; Andy and Jenny Bouma, St. Catharines, Ontario; Rev. John Bylsma, Minneapolis; Rev. Dexter Clark, Phoenix; Rudy De Groot, Calgary, Alberta; Dr. Frank and Janice De Haan, Los Angeles; Gerald Ebbers, Edmonton; Rev. Gerald Frens, Madison, Wisconsin; Rev. Jake Heerema, Grand Rapids, Michigan; Paul and Catharine Heerema, North Haledon, New Jersey; Rev. Gerry Heyboer, Delavan, Wisconsin; Rick Kiekintveld, Graafschap, Michigan; Rev. Peter Kelder, Kenosha, Wisconsin; Rev. Phil Kok, San Diego, California; Rev. Carl Kromminga, Jr., Chicago; Rev. Al Mulder, Chino, California; Mel Persenaire, West Palm Beach, Florida; David and Rhonda Schiebout, Minneapolis; Cliff and Jerilyn Vander Ley, Phoenix; Rev. Rolf Veenstra, Rehoboth, New Mexico; and Rev. Robert Westenbroek, Lake Worth, Florida.

1

The Veldhuisen Family, Emo, Ontario

Brown sugar melts quickly into the ladleful of porridge that Nick Veldhuisen slaps down in the bowl of anyone who happens in for breakfast. The coffee is hot and strong—Canadian strong; it can barely be swallowed black. The eggs are fried in a broad iron skillet, and the children eat their eggs on toast like their father, cutting it up into a hot sandwich, lightly peppered. The raw milk is cold and thick, just brought in from the cooler in the barn. The toast is store-bought, but the light gold honey is from the hives, the same hives that attract the bears. The bears catch the scent of the fresh honey and wander in from the "bush." The bush is the wilderness, and the wilderness sits like a stubborn landlord all around the Veldhuisen dairy.

The Veldhuisens are not an ordinary Christian Reformed family. There are, for instance, seventeen of them in all, including Mom and Dad. Margaret Gertrude came first, in August of '54, and Wilma Jeanette was last, in November of '71. Fifteen children, all healthy, all strong. "Three times," Nick will say, "three times we had to rebuild the kitchen table." Today the rectangular giant stretches the entire width of the kitchen, but there's wasted space at the end. Already seven children are gone—five are married, three of those taking the step in one year. Nick remembers

Johanna Veldhuisen:
instinctively protective of her children.

the sudden change and laughs. "Just over 20 percent," he says; "hardly even noticeable." His dark hair is combed back over his head. After morning milking a few long strands drop toward his ears. He prays beautifully and, when he concludes, the younger children repeat the amen.

Like so many other Canadian Christian Reformed, Nick and his wife, Johanna, "came over" penniless following the Second World War. They came first to Winnipeg; then, following an ethnic railroad of sorts, they arrived in Emo, Ontario, a tiny river town whose "Front Street" faces the Rainy River, borderline between Canada and the States. Today their pennilessness has evolved into a 450-acre farm on the edge of the wilderness—the "bush" as they call it in Emo. Yet only half their land is workable—able to yield the necessary hay for the dairy.

Backpacks and orange nylon tents have made the word *wilderness* quite fashionable these days, but there's little romantic about the bush of northern Ontario. The land is beautiful but not especially hospitable. Moose wander through the cedar swamps. Occasionally, a timber wolf, three feet high at the shoulders, appears from the thin white birch during the long winters, and black bears make startling appearances when the plums ripen in the orchards. Beavers are constantly damming the waterways; the deer and elk make their home in the muskeg, the strange, cushiony soil that feels like an immense waterbed beneath your feet. Red ants build sharp hills that rise from the meadows like Indian mounds. Gerald, the fifth of the boys, says the ants are mean. He steers the tractor between the ant hills on his way to the bush, the loader filled with the innards of a young bull Nick had butchered the night before. "The ants will clean the meat off a carcass in just a few days," he says. Veldhuisen's bush is not a Walt Disney wilderness. Gerald says the bears will rip up what's left of the bull by tomorrow. He dumps the remains no more than a half mile from the house. The Veldhuisens are a wilderness family of seventeen.

And yet they are no different from the rest of the CRC. As strong as it is, the Veldhuisen family has to stretch to cover its generation gaps. They milk thirty cows, keep dozens of chickens, and maintain what most romantically can be referred to as a "family farm." There are three horses, three geese, a turkey or two, dogs, cats, and one bull. But a new Massey-Ferguson stands in the shed; a new baler and a new disc seem somehow out of place. Johanna Veldhuisen smiles defensively when she sees them, remembering many a summer when such luxuries were too extravagant even to covet.

"My son says that someday there will be a new barn and silo here in the pasture," she says. And there's obvious skepticism in her voice, a skepticism fostered by the rigors of the Canadian immigrant experience. She remembers summers when no hay could be put up. She remembers pennilessness as if it were yesterday, and when her own young men see visions and dream dreams, she shows her instinctive protectiveness. "We never believed in buying on credit," she says, remembering only too well those few times when borrowing was the only way to hold on to a fragile dream. That new blue Harvestore her son talks about remains only a dream in his mind. The dairy changes slowly; the new red baler still looks out of place.

And the Veldhuisens feel the conflicts in the church. The Young People have scheduled a dance for their spring retreat. They've asked for it politely, all the churches have been contacted, the consistories have approved (some very reluctantly), and now the first Young Peoples dance will go on. Nick and Johanna wonder if their Mennonite friends and their Baptist friends won't be sure now that the Dutch Reformed are waning in righteousness. They wonder why it is that the children can't create their own entertainment in plays and skits—the way it was always done in the past. They wonder if some of the old ways aren't being sacrificed for something new, something with nothing of the old distinctiveness. And they wonder if the Lord really approves of the dance. It is not an easy issue in Emo; they don't need synod to tell them that much.

Dance or no dance, the spring retreat goes on, and Johanna prays for clear, warm weather. Nick, knowing the land needs rain, teases her for her personal piety. She says she will pray for the needed rain again when the retreat has ended. Nick just shakes his head. It is an old argument. Husband and wife openly admit their differences. The battle will continue.

And then there's this business of evangelism. The Emo church has a considerable number of non-Dutch new members who find it hard to understand the old concerns about Sabbath observance, about dancing, about the necessity of the second service, about so many things that the Veldhuisens, and so many of us, have accepted as part of the confessional heritage of the CRC. And the Veldhuisens know of Christ's mandate to go out and preach; they know that ethnicity has nothing to do with sanctification, but they feel reluctant to concede those old concerns, and who they are, who they always have been, and who they truly feel they should be, in a kind of accommodation to accept and minister to those who don't understand. It is, for the Veldhuisens, and many of us, a very difficult struggle.

One hundred chicks run freely over the yard, next season's source of eggs. Peter, the youngest boy, says that they often get extra chicks because the dealer "can't count a hundred of the little squirts so close." Same thing happens with the turkeys, he says. Peter is thirteen, but when he looks up and says that an extra turkey is worth almost a week of meals to his family, his eyes light up with a mature sense of unmerited blessing far beyond his years. It's a gift from his parents, this familial love and joy. And it's born out of a closeness that seems almost tangible on this dairy in the bush. There are no quiz shows here, no "Sesame Street," not even "The Waltons"—there's no television. The rest of us must decide whether the Veldhuisen family warmth, generated in the coldest area of the North American continent, is a characteristic common to or different from the typical CR family.

Breakfast ends with a reading from *Today*. Nick prays again—for rain, for blessings, for forgiveness of sins, for continued good health. The younger children, as is their custom, echo his amen.

2

Bob Wiers, Principal

If you take North Broadway out of Escondido, California, you will see two schools nestled in the valley not more than a mile from each other.

To your left you will see Escondido High School, a beautifully matched set of one-story buildings placed as perfectly as an architect's drawing, the entire campus spotted with thick green palms. At noon hour, students from Escondido High sit on picnic tables in the wide-open spaces between the buildings, or circle in groups of six or more, munch Twinkies, and sit cross-legged on the well-kept lawn, laughing and joking.

There's a gym, of course, and a fine football field, straight lines of tall bleachers on each side. Somewhere there's a theater with elaborate lighting and a media center where high school students can play with videotapes and Nikon SLR cameras. Escondido High offers an extensive catalog of courses, exotic options, almost unlimited opportunity for high school kids.

Just a bit further down the road, on your right, you will pass Calvin Christian High School, a strong-looking, dark brown brick building, no bigger than any one of the buildings at Escondido High. It has a handsome look, sitting alone on thirteen acres of expensive California real estate, in the background the abrupt, almost muscular hills striped with perfect rows of avocado trees.

There's no athletic field here, just a rough stretch of bleacherless land, bumpy and uneven, where the school's soccer squad sometimes works out. And there's no theater, and no gym, and no media center, and no expensive Nikon SLR cameras. There is just one building—five classrooms and two laboratories, an office, and an all-purpose room no bigger than the fellowship hall of a church. Four kids comprise the entire sophomore class; there are more students in any one of the noon conversations on the Escondido High campus. And the entire student body, twenty-seven students, is no bigger than a sophomore American history class at the school down the road.

If you didn't know a thing about education in the last decade, you might be tempted to question the parental competence of the moms and dads who would opt to send their kids to Calvin Christian, especially in the face of such an obvious disparity in facilities; you would undoubtedly consider such parents to be fanatics of one stripe or another.

But if you have watched as high school placement test scores have fallen off the end of the grid, if you have heard anything about violence and vandalism in the schools, if you know something about public education today—its philosophies, its process—you would know that this new place, Calvin Christian High, is only one of hundreds of alternative high schools begun every year in North America. *Time* reports as many as three new Christian schools per day in the United States alone. If you have been reading *Time,* you might think that Calvin Christian High is, in fine California style, riding the crest of the latest fad—alternative education. But you would still be wrong, dead wrong.

Almost twenty-five years ago, in *One Hundred Years in the New World,* the centennial book of the Christian Reformed Church, John A. Vander Ark, former director of an organization now called Christian Schools International, wrote: "The roots of the Christian school movement are struck into the same soil as the roots of the Christian Reformed Church. . .we must not think of Christian education as an emergence of the last few years nor even of the twentieth century."

Calvin Christian High School is a descendant of a theological tradition thrust into the arena of education. Its ancestral founders have names like Van Prinsterer and Kuyper and Haan and Bavinck and Vander Ark. Its cousin schools educate students in Michigan and Iowa, in Alberta and British Columbia, in Ontario and Bellflower and Ripon, and its philosophical heritage is rooted in phrases like "the covenant," "the kingdom," and "sphere sovereignty." Calvin Christian High has very little to do with trends or fads. Its roots go much deeper.

One needs only to know the principal of Escondido's newest high school to realize its heritage. Bob Wiers is tall and thin, and his sun-streaked hair makes him appear Californian. But he isn't, at least not yet. Bob Wiers, born and reared in Chicago, educated at Trinity Christian College and Calvin College, with a master's from Marquette, has never been a Californian, but he was brought up with an integrated vision of faith and life, a gift from his parents. As far back as he can remember, Bob Wiers was told, by precept and example, that a Christian school is not an alternative to public education, but a necessity. The Escondido people hired him as the school's first principal because his belief is rooted in a tradition, not a fad, and that makes him, even in California, very much of an insider.

"In our school, teachers take the Christian faith and integrate that faith into their studies," he says, sitting in his panelled office in the grade school, a half-block from the new brown high school. "We deal with Christian kids, kids from Christian homes; therefore, our calling is not primarily evangelism, but training students to live as Christians in a fallen world." He says it quietly, assuredly, not as if to create an argument or set the idea in stone tablets. It is, for him, the answer to the question of position—where Calvin Christian stands in the proliferation of alternative schools. "The curriculum here is designed to show the wonders of God the Creator through the lessons of the Christian teacher."

A fad is an emotional thing, really, something which grows when enthusiasm soars. Bob Wiers smiles a lot; it's in his character. But there's no soapbox in his modest office, and he becomes enthusiastic only when he shows off the new classrooms, empty today, and the science lab—the rooms his imagination packs with students, a hundred, even more.

If there are sweeter places than Escondido in North America, you will have to look hard and long to find them. Insulated from the city by a thick green belt comprised of a wildlife sanctuary, a military base, and a mountain range, the Escondido-San Marcos area combines the best of small-town life with easy access to the city, all set in the glories of a California climate—constant sun, dry heat, lush palm trees, Christmas at an ocean beach. More than anyone else, it was Dutch dairy farmers who found the place and who, way back in the mid-50s, organized the church that stands right there with the schools. Others came: construction people from the Midwest, exservicemen who didn't care to leave the San Diego area. The large family trees still line the pews of the sanctuary every Sunday, and it was the families' support that built the brand-new high school.

For close to a decade the board of the elementary school had discussed a high school; for years the society in general had urged them on, approving general plans. When Bob Wiers came to Escondido from Racine, Wisconsin, three years ago, only one question stood between the goals and the first spade of dirt: authority. It is not a unique problem to Escondido. Many Christian Schools International schools provide an education to a diverse student body. In Escondido close to half of the school kids are not from the CRC. As highly as we honor sphere sovereignty—the separation of church and school—it becomes difficult to bequeath power to others when it is the wellsprings of the supporting churches that pump textbooks into classrooms, that allow schools to remain solvent and open.

In Escondido the CRC folk were unwilling to abdicate authority when they knew it was their philosophy and their dollars going in. "We brought a proposal to the society that only people of a Reformed background could be voting members of the society," Bob says. It was, of course, a very conservative position, especially since many society members, mothers and fathers with kids in the grade school, were already exercising voting privileges. "It was an exciting meeting," he remembers, "full of discussion."

But he relied on his own experience in Racine to prove that exclusion from voting membership does not necessarily keep people away from the school. The motion passed. Bob was happy with the position. Hours and hours of parental conferences have taught him that "people from the Reformed persuasion have a broader grasp of what Christian education should be." Just a few years later, in May of 1980, the first spade went down. Three months later, the first classes met their four new teachers in a brand-new building.

But Calvin Christian High does not want to be a "Dutch school." As principal, PR man, parttime teacher, occasional janitor, and chairman of the "Whatever-No-One-Else-Does" Department, Bob takes the whole sophomore class along when he visits the many evangelical elementary schools in the area— Lutheran, Methodist, Baptist. "It just so happens that the three girls in the sophomore class sing beautifully together," he says. "We should be paying them for the work they do for the school. But it's a neat feeling they have for the place—all of these first kids. They know

Bob Wiers:
an insider from Racine, Wisconsin.

they're the first, that they're making history, and it creates a feeling for the school that you just wouldn't believe. They're really special to us."

One year nearly completed, Bob is sure that the school will grow, that others from other churches will be coming. "It's a bandwagon effect, even with some of our own people. It seems like a big risk right away—just four sophomores—but now the school is there—you can see it. Community people are going to come. We're getting some already. Our grade school has a strong reputation for quality Christian education. The others will come here too." There's determination in his voice, determination rooted in conviction, not just emotion.

Not more than a year ago, Bob Wiers flew back to Chicago, leaving his wife, Judy, and two small children in California for what he knew would be a short time. His father, just sixty-five, was dying of cancer. He didn't look forward to the end, not until he got there. There was an inevitable sense of his father's passing; but rather than burden them, imminent death freed them—father, son Bob, and son Rog, a history teacher at Illiana Christian High. "We got time to talk, to remember the stories of our childhood with him. We had time to thank him for a Christian education," he says, "because it shaped us into what we are today. And it was costly to him; we weren't that wealthy."

Bill Wiers, a retired Chicago truck driver, died in the company of his family on a Sunday night. "Actually it was a spiritual high, to experience joy from what I had really expected to be a horrible situation," Bob says, easily.

Today, in beautiful Escondido, when Bob Wiers walks from the grade school to the high school, he sometimes catches the reflection of his rolling walk in the windows that face North Broadway. "I laugh," he says, "because I look just like my dad."

Bob Wiers, principal of Calvin Christian High School, is the picture of his father in some ways. He is

25

the product of a familial tradition, of a covenant promise, and of a backbone philosophy of the school and the church and the community he serves.

Working out God's Word in his professional life as principal, Bob Wiers is what the dairy farmers, the construction bosses, the mothers and fathers of Escondido want in their own children. He may be no Californian, but he's an insider, and that's why they've hired him for the new school on North Broadway.

3

Grandma Los

The living room of Hattie Los's home is little more than a cubicle; the ceiling is low and the dark brown paneling shows that someone has tried to make one-hundred-year-old plaster walls look suburban. It's the kind of place where you might guess a great-grandmother would live—there's not a right angle in the house.

Grandma Los lives alone, but the room is crowded with chairs—straight chairs, a captain's chair, maybe a rocker, a sofa, and at least one big soft one in the corner opposite the TV stand. All the chairs are for Sunday, of course, for that one hour after church when her children, and their children, and their children's children drop by for a "goodie."

Paint-by-number landscapes line the walls. "Pete did those," she says. Pete was Mr. Los. He died just a few months before their sixty-third wedding anniversary. There's a card from President Ford on the china cabinet, framed, a picture of the President pasted on it. "That was for our sixtieth," she says. "Cut the picture out of *The Banner*." Hattie Los smiles continuously, but when she talks about her Pete, her smile brightens even more. "He's dead now, two years. He's where he always hoped he'd be someday," she says.

Just outside of Grandma Los's kitchen window stands

a massive oak, strong and dignified, its gnarled branches and twigs grown in a thousand crooked angles; yet, somehow, all together, they create a nearly perfect circle above the thick, proud trunk. And it's an old tree, full of stories probably—if trees could talk—stories of how the men once laid the brick that makes your tires grumble when you drive down the main street of Delavan, Wisconsin. It's a scrub oak, a second-class oak, the kind of oak that's not as clean, perhaps not as pure, as its cousin oak trees. But it's straight and strong.

Oak was once the wood of the people. Few midwestern families had kitchen tables that weren't cut from open-grained oak. Hard wood. Wood that could put up with years of coffee, dinners, coffee, suppers, generations of milk-spillers, entire lifetimes. Grandma Los's scrub oak is that kind of oak. In early October it ignites as if set afire by a natural torch, turning yellow and orange and brown in a spectacular ritual that only Grandma Los could recount exactly. As beautiful as it is in the late spring, its green leaves unfurled in the warm southern breezes, autumn is the scrub oak's showcase.

Grandma Los—almost everyone calls her "Grandma" —is, in her own way, not so much different from that big oak outside her window. She's over eighty now, brimming with stories. She doesn't get out to church anymore; but she listens to tapes of four sermons every week, two from the local preacher, two from her son in Michigan. Her rheumatoid arthritis has swelled her joints, all of them, with stiffness, and her lumpy hands portray her lifelong battle, her fingers thick and angular like the branches of the scrub oak. "But I do just fine," she says, her left hand patting the arm of her wheelchair. "Aspirin keeps the pain down," she says, smiling, as always, "and I don't feel it at all like in the old days." She raises her hands in front of her face, touching her fingers pointer to pointer in a kind of gesture. "When I was fifteen, I spent three months in bed while it just spread from one place to another. Couldn't even get up." Later, she and her husband had nine children. "But you know," she says, "that whole time I was never bothered by it, not until I was close to fifty. Nine children. Pete on the farm. All the kids. And I was just as active as anybody. That's a miracle."

Hattie Los had to be active. Hattie Los's story is a chronicle of American history: a South Dakota childhood, her parents an immigrant Frisian couple, the Logtermans of Springfield; married before she was twenty to Peter Los, son of a good, middle-class merchant from Leiden, the only member of a strong family to feel any urge for the adventure of a new country. "I will be back in five years," Pete had told his family when he left in 1911. Then came the war. Then he met Hattie. He finally did return, but not until after World War II when both mother and father had recently died. There was no medicine during the occupation.

During the 30s, Hattie and Pete spent too many precious farm hours sweeping up dust from the kitchen, shaking it out of the quilts, spanking it out of the children's filthy clothes every night, and every night sweeping a pailful up from inside the home. "We saw it coming when we left church one Sunday. It looked maybe like rain," she says. "I had left my children's clothes on the bed, you know, for them to change after church. When I came upstairs, I could barely see them on the bed, there was so much dust already." It was new to them and therefore scary, because they didn't know what was happening. Soon they knew. Dust took over the farm like a snarling landlord, choking the machinery, blinding the livestock. South Dakota became a dust bowl.

They watched grasshoppers devour the crops made frail by the dust and searing prairie winds. "It was over 100 degrees in March," she says. "And the land had been so good before. We didn't know what was

Grandma Los:
living and loving on the plains.

happening. The hoppers ate everything later, even the onions in the ground."

They were rescued by Roosevelt's New Deal, Pete given jobs that brought them enough money for clothes and food for their growing family.

The Los family lived with the Sioux on the Rosebud Reservation. They made friends with dark-skinned people with non-Frisian names like No Good. They traded bread and butter, eggs and meat, for the Indians' government surplus handouts, clothing that seemed ridiculous to the Indians: wool army coats, buckle boots, hats. They watched other whites, even whites from their own church, take advantage of the Sioux: steal the horses the Indians let run and cheat them out of what they deserved for the fence posts they would cut from the river and bring up to the farmers for trade.

While Pete's Dutch nephews risked their lives hiding from conscription into Hitler's Nazi army, the Los family gave up a son—and brother—to the war effort of the Allies. Frank, twenty-five, the second of the boys, already the father of two children, was killed in December of 1944, the month of his birthday, very soon after digging his first foxhole in European earth. The story of Hattie Los is a course in American history.

Hattie Los has lived through what she has because she's strong. She's a powerful woman, even today in a wheelchair. Her shoulders are broad and square, her arms still thick as heavy branches. Her hair is white, and little wisps of silver curl out from beneath the hair net over the back of her head. Her eyes are clear and fresh behind the rectangular glasses she wears when she reads from the pile of books lying next to her big soft chair. And her features, her nose and mouth, seem almost muscular—the kind of face, the kind of woman, really, who could live on the plains in the very bad years, the kind of woman who could love on the plains in the very bad years.

31

"I can cry easy," she says, "both from being sad and being happy." Not long ago, in one Sunday morning service, Grandma Los saw three grandchildren baptized and two make public profession of faith. "I was filled up with joy," she says. "I could have cried." The threat of tears is in her eyes when she remembers that Sunday, but the threat's there, too, the moment she mentions those of her family who don't care for the church. "I can cry easy," she says again, but when she tells her stories, one realizes that *easy* is not the right word. Grandma Los was a farm wife, a South Dakota prairie woman, a strong Frisian, a mother who delivered seven of her own nine children with the help of her husband and sometimes a midwife. Grandma Los feels deeply, but she really doesn't cry easy.

"But it hurts," she says, when she talks of those other grandchildren, brought up in the church, graduated from the local Christian school, former students at denominational colleges, those grandchildren today rejecting the church, even neglecting their Lord. She says it hurts her that her grandchildren can go to Calvin or Dordt and then not care. She prays for the colleges. She says that our church is only as strong as our colleges. "It starts in the colleges," she says, her hands out in front of her, constantly moving. "They got to teach the right principles, the right religion," she says, even her rheumatic shoulders pumping when she talks.

"Maybe I'm here yet to pray for my grandchildren," she explains, her smile brightening again. "That's my privilege."

Perhaps every Christian Reformed church doesn't have a Grandma Los. If so, then some are not so blessed as Delavan.

The autumn winds are tearing at the leaves of the scrub oak. But the tree is beautiful now, this October, resplendent in the fire of the season, almost confident in the ominous threat of another midwestern winter.

Not so much different from Grandma Los really. She faces no such winter. She faces only eternal spring, better than the warmest May afternoon in Delavan. She knows it. And that's what lights her smile, a smile of more than eighty years of life.

4

Siep Drexhage

Before she was old enough for school, Siep Heeringa knew that her mother disliked Indonesia, coming to the place only because her husband, a self-made man from Friesland, had wanted to make the move.

Her father advanced himself in Indonesia; his strong, authoritative way brought him up quickly into police administration. There would have been no such chance for him in Delft, where her mother and father had met and where Jaap Heeringa had been only a groom, and later a guard, in the police cavalry. In the port city of Soerabaja, Indonesia, Jaap made a fine living for his family and found freedom from the regimentation of life in Holland.

But Siep's mother was, as they said in Malaysian, *blanda tottok,* or thoroughly Dutch. She hated the dirt, her fair skin burned in the 115° heat, and the deep earthquakes shook her family too often to suit her. She missed her native Delft terribly.

But in spite of her dislike for Indonesia, Bep Heeringa always found time for the naked Indonesian children, even when other Dutch people thought the attention she paid them excessive. Siep's mother would point toward the curious native children wandering around the open church. "Come, sit," she would tell them in their language from her own seat on the breezy edge of the sanctuary. Some thought it an unnecessary disruption of worship.

Siep watched her mother, and, when she was only six years old, her mind was already a notebook of memories —she recalls the gifts of candy and toys her mother would make to the children at Christmas. She saw in her mother the strange confluence of compassion for a people and distaste for a region, balancing somehow. It created a vivid image within her, something today as much a part of her as her speech or her step or the strength she has built to cover and protect other inescapable images of a past freighted with the inhumanities of war.

One afternoon in 1941, when the heavy sirens wailed through the streets of Soerabaja, nine-year-old Siep Heeringa knew that this was no practice run. Everyone knew the Japanese were coming, and this time, sitting at her desk in the public school, Siep was sure, somehow, that this was the hour she had feared ever since she and her friends had been evicted from the School with the Bible so that the army could mount anti-aircraft guns on the flat roof.

She had hated the new public school, and when, this time, the awful sirens warned of an air attack, one thought obsessed her and pushed her like an instinct: I will not die here—I will not! Confusion scattered her classmates as the shouting teachers tried to usher them toward the school shelter. Siep could think only of her bicycle and escape. When she veered from the phalanx of children, no one saw her, and when her legs churned at the pedals, her little body working against the soft asphalt almost melting in the heat, no one witnessed her pedaling for her life.

The streets of the city turned dumb. Around her nothing moved—everyone, everything, burrowing into dirt-covered shelters. Soerabaja turned speechless with fear, the neighborhoods quarantined by an unseen but imminent plague of single-engined horror. Siep's body nearly quit as her thin legs battled the pedals.

And she wasn't surprised when she heard the horrible slow bass drone of the planes, like the lowest note of a great pipe organ. She knew they were coming. When her breath was all but gone, pure instinct drove her legs. Finally, just two blocks from home, a man appeared and pushed her along on the bike.

And then the planes were there, the pointed popping of the machine guns strafing the Java dust, spitting tongues of dirt all around her in razor-sharp lines of fire. In her mind she saw her own back torn by lead, her white blouse matted with blood. The neighbor man pushed her down into her own family's shelter, and she fell at the entrance, her body's strength depleted.

When her mother heard the sudden noise outside the shelter, she flashed images of parachuting Japanese soldiers. Full of fear, Siep's mother grabbed a long kitchen knife and edged outside to protect her family.

Siep saw the long knife when she heard her mother cry, the bombs hitting around them.

There were no more battles in Soerabaja; the surrender was a fearful, foregone conclusion. When her father heard the announcement on the radio, he cried because he knew there would be no escape. All hope simply faded for her then; to see her strong father, the provider and protector, broken by the news was to feel the end of hope. The enemy surrounded them and lived in them like a parasite. As a member of the local militia, her father was taken first. He was taken to a distant labor camp.

Her mother was left alone in the omnipresence of an enemy both capable of and prone to kill indiscriminately. To feed the family, Bep Heeringa turned into a sharp business dealer, turning the hallowed Sunday front room into a shop and her children into delivery boys and girls on bicycles.

Then, with little warning, the Japanese took the rest of the family. One day her mother, beaten about the face and chest, returned on a bike. "We must be gone

Siep Drexhage:
wearing a gift from the Indo-Chinese refugees
she helped settle in Edmonton, Alberta.

in a half hour," she told her four children. "Take only what you can carry." A year later in the work camp, she told them they would have been shot had they reported late to the camp; she had been told as much by the guard who had butted her in the chest with his rifle.

When they arrived at the camp, they were herded as a family into a tiny cubicle dwelling with a single entrance. Siep's mother, afflicted for years with a peculiar heart disorder, went into a kind of cardiac arrest triggered by the tension. The children carried her onto a mattress in the back corner of the shack. They were afraid; the idea of their mother dying and deserting them there threatened them more than the rifles, the samurai swords, the rigid commands.

In the hills of Java, all four seasons appear in a single day, the afternoon heat dissipating into a gripping night cold. When Siep's brother tried to light a gas burner, the entire shack exploded into flame, the fire snapping like a dragon between the children and their helpless mother. Together they pushed through the flames and carried her heavy body out, dropping her outside on the ground and stanching the fire that clung to her dress. Siep, just twelve years old, thought sure her mother would die. She didn't.

But slowly and inevitably her mother's strength diminished. Siep knew her own role as provider had to grow in proportion to her mother's weakness, so she worked her way into the kitchen crew, a long and difficult detail that gave her opportunities to pocket extra food for her family, especially her seven-year-old brother. "I knew that if anyone would have touched him, I would have been fully capable of killing to protect him," she admits today.

The camp's cooking drums became a source of food. Siep would jump in to clean them out; once inside she would jam handfuls of rice into the pockets or folds of her dress, bringing it home to hungry kids later that night.

Her mother's condition continued to deteriorate. The chest wounds she had received from the earlier beating were infected. The Dutch nurses realized that Bep Heeringa needed to find the kind of medical help the Japanese wouldn't provide for her in the camp. Somehow, the guards allowed her to go to an Indonesian hospital outside of the camp, a place where students used human beings for practice. But there was no choice, really. She told her children that she would die for sure if she were to stay in the camp. "At least I'll have a chance," she told them the night before she left.

The children had no idea where she went, and they heard nothing from her for weeks. In time, they began to assume that she was dead, and at night, locked in their room, they missed their mother.

"Heeringa! Heeringa!" The cry split through the walls of the shack in the middle of the night. "It's your mother." They had been sure she was dead. Curfew or not, the children charged from the shack.

"There she was," Siep remembers today. "It was a miracle." The doctors had taken half of the breast away, cutting through the infection, making it spread even more quickly. "But she had walked all the way— miles and miles—with an open chest." She brought each of the children little gifts, after trading her food for money or trinkets. "I thought she was dead," Siep says today. "I was delirious."

But it was just a matter of time. Her mother's body weakened rapidly under the power of the relentless infection. She could not eat. "In all that time she never once complained—not once," Siep says. "She wanted badly to see my father, but through all that, she never was bitter against God." She continually tried to perk up others in the makeshift hospital of the war camp— making others smile, other women without food or medicine, other women waiting, like she was, to die alone, husbandless, in the hills of Java.

"She just refused to die," Siep remembers. But finally her spirit relented to a ravaged body long ago marked for death.

"That night was a difficult time," she says, "and I don't like to dwell on it. It goes beyond words."

Siep Drexhage is a strong-looking woman, and her hair is still curly like it was so long ago when she pedaled her bicycle down the streets of Soerabaja. When she thinks about the camps, when she remembers that war experience and talks of it, her face changes expressions quickly to reflect the assault of intense emotions she carries like a scrapbook of her first fifteen years. The war did it. The war turned despair into ecstasy in a second, and then pushed joy out with immediate, unexpected horror. It distorted the normal range of emotions—fear of death or humiliation, love of family, the will to live—and stretched a person's feelings into what seems the grotesque: the subhuman disregard of human need, the superhuman will to provide and to exist. The record of the war is written today in the intensity of the smiles and frowns on Siep Drexhage's face.

They buried their mother in the war camp in the hills of Java.

"For a long time I was bitter about things, bitter that God had taken away the one whom I trusted and loved completely. I was not an easy child. My mother was, at the time, the only one who accepted and understood me. But I learned that bitterness was something like being self-centered. I was shocked by naive people whose major concern was matching the colors of a lampshade to their pillow cases." She speaks with the confidence of someone who knows that certain things are packed away neatly behind her. "The bitterness went away when I started being aware of other people. I'm convinced of that now—the only way to conquer bitterness is to get your thoughts away from yourself."

That lesson took several years of immigrant Canadian life, a good marriage to Gerry Drexhage, and four sons, all healthy. Finally, that lesson took the applied example of a mother whose love and loyalty and faith stand as a testimony, a mother whose body lies in an unmarked grave in the Java hills, but whose soul is with her God. That woman's memory is a legacy, an inspiration, and a standard.

The legacy of Siep's mother can be heard today in the staccato phone conversations Siep keeps up quite regularly. "Ja, Chong, you come my house tonight. We talk. You come tonight. Eight o'clock."

"Ja, Chong. You come. Tonight. We talk."

The sound of the samurai sword dragging in the hard rock dust, the beastly crackling laughter of the camp guards, the smell of constant personal humiliation—none of that has kept Siep Drexhage from her avocation today—the relocation of Indo-Chinese refugees. She has, in a biblical pattern, found herself amid the needs of others.

So today Siep's friend Chong, in some apartment in Edmonton, is having trouble with the landlord. He wants to talk to "Mrs. Siep" because she has shown love and loyalty and faith in the past, like her own mother once did, like her own mother would have done today.

5

Bill and Nelle Wanders, Phoenix, Arizona

Bill and Nelle Wanders haven't forgotten their childhood and the days when churchgoing was an all-day affair. They would pack their bread and sardines—the Wanders and the Roozebooms and the other farm families around Tracy, Iowa—and head for town and the little wooden Christian Reformed church below the tracks. The church family was basically Groenendyks, Roozebooms, and Hoksbergens, plus a few strays from nearby central Iowa hamlets.

In the 1920s and 30s some would take cars, some would take horses, but the farm families would usually spend the whole day at church, the women setting coffee in the consistory room, the children munching down the sandwiches while sitting on the long, wooden benches of the sanctuary. While the mas and pas were busy visiting over coffee, the kids would take long walks along the railroad tracks by the church. Safely out of sight of the parents, a few naughty boys would sometimes toss a ball around during the short hours between the morning and afternoon services.

Then everyone would reassemble for the second service. The Wanders remember Sundays because Sunday was, simply, the biggest day of the week in rural Iowa.

Sunday night was Young Peoples and Tuesday

night, catechism. When formal schooling ended for most kids at the eighth grade, those nights rose out of the weekly calendar of farm work like the first hint of spring after a long prairie winter. Nelle Roozeboom stopped shucking corn with her brother and headed into town, and Bill Wanders made sure he had all the chores done with an hour or so to spare. "You missed a Tuesday night," he remembers, "and you felt real bad."

Sometimes on Sunday nights the young kids would sneak over to the "holy roller" church. "We didn't make any fun or anything," Bill says, "but it was just so different that you might say it was entertainment, watching them roll over the bales of hay."

It was a natural thing when Bill and Nelle started seeing each other, right around the beginning of the Second World War. After all, they were both eligible for the kind of courting that normally occurred in and around Tracy, and it was, after all, no mixed marriage. Nelle's mother had warned her often that she shouldn't think of marrying an "American." And Bill's father was even an elder. Bill and Nelle must have looked like a handsome couple to the church below the tracks.

Today the Wanders's front porch faces the recently remodeled Phoenix, Arizona, Christian Reformed Church, the church the Wanders both attend and vacuum every week. The nearest horses are probably a long way off, standing in stalls at the racetracks or lugging overweight Easterners at some desert dude ranch. The Wanders live just a block or so from 24th Street, a busy, four-lane crosstown that is lined with the American smorgasbord of fast-food restaurants— Pizza Huts, McDonald's and Kentucky Frieds, plus a Dunkin' Donuts for Sunday mornings. Their world has changed some over the years.

Alvin Toffler has made a fortune writing about the very changes the Wanders see and feel. His first book, *Future Shock,* warned readers in the early 70s that few of us would be prepared for the computer age and the post-industrial world. Recently, his book *The Third Wave* has taken a more optimistic, long view, claiming that abrupt and violent upheaval, seen in perspective, may allow us to visualize a new and glorious civilization.

But Bill and Nelle Wanders don't put much stock in Alvin Toffler. Bill and Nelle put their trust in an old tent of the Calvinist faith they were reared on in the Tracy Christian Reformed Church—God's sovereignty. Talk to the Wanders for a while, sit with them in the calm, spring warmth of an Arizona morning, listen to the delicate wind chimes hung from the front porch that faces the church, and God's sovereignty and his will chorus from the conversation as regularly as the refrain of an old, favorite hymn.

"Many of us have to face what I call a Gethsemane experience," Bill says; "the Lord brings us to specific times to point out to us that what is happening is out of our control. Those times bring us to our knees. It's then you say, 'Lord, not my will, but your will be done.'" Those realizations are not easy to make because they demand a denial of our own power, a confession that in ourselves we are powerless. For many of us, depravity is a fine doctrine; we may even like to hear it preached. But few of us, perhaps, like to admit that we run solely on God's power. It's much more exciting to think that we have our own generators.

Bill Wanders's Gethsemane occurred in the middle of a choir anthem in the church across the street. "We thank you, Lord, for love so strong and true"—that's what he was singing when it struck him. Bill and Nelle had been agonizing over their children, like so many parents, anxious and worried because they feared their kids were leaving the paths that they had set for them. "I had to go out of church right in the middle of the song because it all hit me clearly. I was not thanking the Lord at all; I was rebelling—I was angry because

Bill Wanders:
both attending and vacuuming
the Phoenix CRC every week.

Nelle Wanders:
all lies are big lies.

God didn't seem to be living up to his promises. And then I realized that I was trying to tell the Lord what to do with my life and my kids' lives also."

It's a common error for all of us, of course, substituting our will for His. And it's a subtle form of depravity, not as interesting or public as fornication or drunkenness, but just as much a sin and very much more pervasive. Pride, the medievalists say, is the first of the seven deadly sins.

A Gethsemane is never a sweet experience; before new life grows, "the old man of sin" must die in a pattern not unlike the myth of the phoenix bird. But a real Gethsemane experience is liberating because it frees one from the onerous burden of total personal responsibility. It teaches reliance and perseverence. It bestows comfort in God's sovereign power.

Bill and Nelle have five children; the only boy, John, preaches in the Marysville (Washington) Cascade Christian Reformed Church, but the others have all left the CRC for other denominations. "You could say it hurt us some," Nelle says. "It disappointed us a lot, but we came to understand it and to trust in the will of God." There's that phrase again, as if you hadn't heard it before.

"We've learned that the body of Christ isn't all hands or feet. Some denominations stress different things—youth programs, neighborhood evangelism—and God used all of them to fulfill his plan." Considering the ethnic purity of the Tracy CRC, the Dutch church of their youth, and considering the old doctrinaire admonitions against the Methodists and the "Americans," the Wanders have adjusted to their new world, and they have not suffered "future shock." They've learned an old lesson that Toffler doesn't offer—to sacrifice their own will. They've learned to trust.

But submission doesn't mean withdrawal, nor does it imply a "laid back" Christianity. It doesn't mean an end to suffering. Anxiety still arises in unforeseen ways. Recently, the Wanders did some grocery shopping in a local supermarket. Nelle picked out a 25¢ card for her kids' anniversary and slipped it into her open purse to keep it away from the perspiring milk cartons in the grocery cart. Thirty dollars' worth of groceries later, she had forgotten the card, and she walked out of the store, the card, unpaid for, still in her open purse.

As if out of nowhere, the store detective took her elbow and ushered her to his desk in the back of the stockroom. "We'll be done in a flash, lady. Just stay calm," he told her. He snapped some Polaroid shots of her and scribbled "shoplifter" at the bottom in dark, thick letters. The man was deaf to her protests. "I didn't mean to do it," she said. "I will go back and pay for it." He had heard the line before, he told her. He had her cold, out of the store, the card in her purse, unpaid for.

"Something like that happens to you and you start questioning yourself. You can't sleep," Nelle says. The experience is still fresh in her mind; there hasn't been time for a scar to form.

A polygraph test was the only way out for her. Pass the lie detector test and the charge is dropped, store officials told her. But nothing in her Tracy background had prepared her for the angst of the polygraph. Tape pulled securely around her fingers and head, a band around her elbow, she remembers feeling as if she were going to die right there. "All they would have had to do was slip a bag over my head, and turn a switch, and I just figured I was gone," she says. "It was a bad experience."

"From when you were a child until you were forty-five, did you ever lie, Mrs. Wanders?" the man said. She was told to face the wall, not to look at the questioner, not to turn her head, to answer only yes or no.

To someone reared like Nelle Roozeboom Wanders,

all lies are lies. She told him she had lied to her mother when she was a girl, when her mother asked her if she had done something she was accused of.

"I mean a big lie," the man told her from behind.

To Nelle Wanders, all lies are big lies.

She failed the polygraph.

Their pastor wanted to call a congregational meeting, but the Wanders, advised by a lawyer and their children, lined up a string of character witnesses—a local politician from the church and others. The store gave them another chance—another polygraph—but the Wanders's lawyer insisted that it be administered by an objective consultant, not store officials.

This time she passed. After five minutes in preliminary hearing the 25¢ shoplifting charge was dropped from the books, cleared completely. But not until those incriminating "shoplifter" mug shots were returned did Nelle feel it was finally over. Two long months of uncertainty, of anguish, of shame, even of guilt, finally lifted.

"The Lord works through those things too," Bill says. You can't help but wonder immediately how he can tailor theology to cover this story. "It brought us closer together," she says. "We told each other things, confided in each other, like we hadn't before." Bill lays a hand on Nelle's shoulder.

Bill and Nelle Wanders have been married for thirty-eight years; they have raised five children; they have fourteen grandchildren. They have worked together on the farm in Tracy, as church janitors, as yard-keepers and housekeepers, and you can't help but wonder whether anything could have been left unsaid in all that shared time. But when they sit together on their front porch, facing the church, and smile like newlyweds, you can't question their testimony.

This summer, like every other summer since 1960, when they left the farm in Tracy, the Wanders will pack their VW bus and head east—"back home"—

back to the rest of the family, the Wanders and the Roozebooms. "I guess it's the *Wanders* in me that loves to travel," Bill says. They've found over fifteen routes to get back and forth to Iowa, but this year they will probably discover something new. They'll be alone, of course, their children all married and settled, the four daughters keeping up their weekly Bible study together, their son preaching in Washington. It will be just Bill and Nelle and the God whose will they've learned to serve in some sixty years of changes that seem sometime minuscule in the presence of their sovereign, eternal Father.

6

Professor Wayne R. Tinga, University of Alberta

Maybe one of the accomplishments that Dr. Wayne Tinga most treasures is the fact that, in nearly twenty years as a Young Peoples leader in the Edmonton area, he has not once been dumped into the icy waters of any Alberta lake. Not once. And that's as much a statement of fact as a challenge—if any Edmonton young people are out there listening. He's been active in the church's ministry to its kids ever since he was a kid himself, way back in the mid-50s, when his family immigrated; he says he figures he never really outgrew the organization. In those years he's been through nearly as many retreats and conventions as Jim Lont. And he's never been dunked. Never. Get the hint?

Wayne Tinga, now a few Young Calvinist conventions past forty years old, could probably pass for a kid himself. He has a youthful face, reddish-blond, short-cut hair that hangs neatly over his forehead, and a wiry frame that makes him look like a lightweight high school wrestler or a quick defenseman on the church hockey team.

But he isn't a kid. Dr. Wayne R. Tinga, christened Wiebe Roelof Tinga in Leeuwarden, Friesland, is a Ph.D. in electrical engineering and professor at the University of Alberta. His curriculum vita reads like a graduate textbook in engineering, but the titles of his publications mean very little to anyone who hasn't mastered microwaves, as Professor Tinga has: for instance, "Generalized Approach to Multiphase Dielectric Mixture Theory," appearing in the September 1973 volume of the *Journal of Applied Physics*, or "Effects of Microwave on Periplaneta Americana and Tribolium Confusum," published way back in 1966, just after he had completed his master's degree at the University of Alberta. There are a couple dozen such entries on his publication list, and what that list illustrates is the expertise of Dr. Tinga, a world authority on microwaves, former chairman of the board of governors of the Internation Microwave Power Institute, an organization of research scientists representing over twenty-five countries. His research lab on campus is as full of microwave ovens as a Sears outlet —several different varieties in several states of repair, some partly dismantled, some mechanical guinea pigs —the subjects of Wayne Tinga's ongoing research in the power and uses of microwaves.

His love for tinkering he inherited from his father, a baker by profession but an inventor by inclination. "Way back when I was a kid, I remember collecting lead all over the city, then hauling it up to a bedroom in our house in Leeuwarden," he says. There, the Tinga family turned into an assembly line, melting down the lead, then, pouring it into a mold his father had created, and producing heavy stands for long-stemmed flowers, leaded display fonts the Tinga enterprise sold to Frisian florists.

He remembers taking apart his bicycle out front on the sidewalk when he was seven or eight years old, once a week at least, cleaning it up when it hadn't accumulated even a speck of dirt; he was always much more interested in the process and the materials—the nuts and bolts, the axles, the grease. And he once strung a telephone wire from the first to the third floor of his childhood home, creating a two-way communication system between basement and attic.

But he never dreamed of being an engineer; in Holland there was little opportunity, anyway, of becoming one. When the Tinga family immigrated in 1953, Wayne was taken out of the vocational track schooling he was put into in Leeuwarden and brought into the more free system of public education in Canada.

Even today, in his second-floor office in the Department of Electrical Engineering, he seems to find it difficult to imagine how it was he came to be a professor. If anything, it was a mistake, at least as human beings plot the courses of their lives. Wayne knows there was a plan. Challenged by an engineering prof during a high school career day, he decided to enroll in an engineering program, sure that an engineer was a rugged outdoors type who hung from utility poles or built complicated machinery in the bush, somewhere in the Alberta wilds. Somehow, he never got there, and today, the university exam period just concluded, he stares at an uncorrected pile of written exams from undergraduates as if the whole story were some kind of humorous miscalculation.

But he loves his work. "Money has never been the important factor in choosing my work," he says. "I've always felt that doing interesting things that could benefit mankind was the most important consideration for me." Most anybody could say something like that; few could really mean it. A line like that could seem some kind of sanctimonious subterfuge, but in Wayne Tinga's case it isn't. The proof is clear in the designs he dreams for the future.

Today, despite the length of his publication list, he admits that microwaves don't excite him as much as they once did. "I'm convinced that a greater utilization of microwaves in homes could reduce energy consumption," he says, "but it seems that everything we've done has only been an additional convenience for the rich. The price of the microwave oven is still prohibitive, and the production and marketing is still heavily geared toward conventional cooking." When he says it, his eyes scan the oven models that surround him like so much paraphernalia.

He may feel slightly disenchanted on the basis of his experience as a microwave consultant. Since 1968, Dr. Tinga has hired himself out to major corporations and institutions for investigation of the possibilities of microwave usage in everything from US Army field kitchens to neighborhood donut bakeries, for everything from the processing of automobile parts to the treatment of nuclear waste.

But more likely, his slight dissatisfaction arises from his faith. Wayne Tinga knows better than most that the potential for microwave power is no longer limitless with present technology. On the basis of his own confession, he admits that there are other ways in which his expertise can serve his God and his neighbor more fully than through microwave research.

If you want to see him excited, talk computers. To Tinga personally, computers are a whole new area, but they are an exciting and promising technological development whose immediate and long-range future holds far more potential benefit than microwaves for the man and woman on the street. Ironically, it was while spending nearly a year in Minneapolis as a consultant to Litton Industries, building a prototype of his own patented microwave oven, that the potential for the computer appeared to him. The complexity of the required electronics led him to use microcomputers in his design, and their use prompted him to think more specifically about the use of computers in research, especially by noncomputer experts. Today his most prized research is in programming the computer to observe experiments and take measurements that research assistants formerly had to do, spending untold hours in tedious and often incidental note-taking.

This notable shift in professional interest, only midway through a career that had already brought him in-

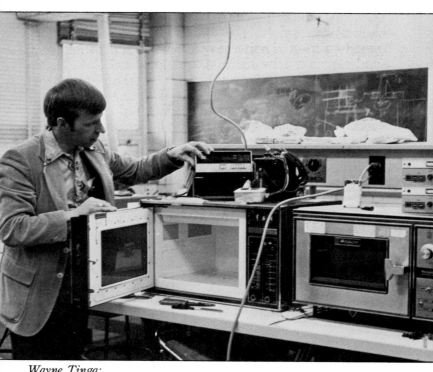

Wayne Tinga:
dreaming for the future.

ternational recognition, is proof of his confession: he wishes to use his gifts to benefit people. His forceful way, his manner of using his hands when he speaks, his forthright references to his Creator, all of those underline his belief and fortify his testimony. He is, first of all, a committed, industrious man of faith.

"We were taught to be workers, right from the start," he says, and to understand the force of the early education he describes, one needs to feel something of the effect of the German occupation during the Second World War. Wayne Tinga was just two years old when the first Nazi troops stood in groups on the street corners of his hometown, and he was just six when the mammoth Allied tanks, packed full of green-shirted Canadians throwing out chocolate bars, rumbled down the tiny city streets like loving metallic monsters and freed them all from five long years of physical and mental torture.

"I remember the German occupation very well," he says, despite the fact that it started and ended before he was old enough to learn to read. "You grew up quickly," he says, and the testimony of the narratives he spins illustrates the vividness of the images, planted so early and still rooted there, locked back in his memory like some latent madness in a conscious world now so far removed from black markets and informers and work camps and imminent death.

As children, the Tingas learned to be on the lookout for German patrols. Routinely, the Nazis would search homes, hoping to find able-bodied men and boys to fill the ranks of workers at munitions factories in Germany. Routinely, the Dutch families would lie to protect a father or brother hiding in some attic hideaway. Wayne Tinga's father spent most of the years of the occupation out of sight, unable even to attend church on many Sundays of the year.

Perhaps one incident may illustrate the emotional flailing taken by the Dutch during the occupation. It happened one night when the Tingas were unaware of the Nazi patrol heading down their street. Wayne's father sat in a chair in the front room when the soldiers hammered on the door. There was no chance for him to escape to his hiding place, and he could not leave the safety of the house. In a moment the Nazis were in the door. Wayne's mother played idiot to stall for time, while his father stood at the window and wound the curtains around his body, hoping not to be found in the room-to-room search which would inevitably follow. Wayne, just five years old, barely old enough to tie his own shoes, sat and watched the drama, already convinced that his father would be taken away from him and his brothers and sisters, possibly forever. He knew it because he saw his father's shoes sticking out from under the drapes like a horrible joke. A German corporal stared down at his father's shoes beneath the curtains. Wayne watched the German's eyes mark the very spot, then swing back to his. His own life seemed suddenly fatherless.

The commanding officer stepped in, and the child's heart raged.

"There is no one here," the corporal said. The officer took the corporal's word, and the Nazis left without a man. Wayne Tinga's father stepped from behind the curtain, free. The boy who had lost a father had been given him back miraculously, a lifetime of despair and joy in a drama of thirty seconds.

"It was good for me to see that," he says today, "because I learned that I shouldn't hate Germans. This guy blinded himself to Dad's presence. It was something else I had to hate, not just Germans."

It was a marvelous lesson in the crossfire of hate and devotion, in the reality of both death and life, a lesson far beyond the range of a kindergarten curriculum. But more than that, the compression of emotions in that front-room drama—the shock of a totally unforeseen Nazi denial, the surety of terrible loss miraculously changed to elation, fear turned to joy, love wrenched out of hate—the battery of conflicting, intense emotions triggered in just seconds within the mind and heart and soul of a five-year-old boy matured him beyond childishness and gave him a childlike faith which all his education and all his advanced research has not taken from him.

"I remember thinking that the Lord's Hand must have been there," he says. God manifested himself as a nearly tangible reality, a real character in the everyday life of a five-year-old boy. " 'God is here; he is protecting us,' I thought."

And it is that kind of reality that firms the resolve and shapes the commitment of Wayne Tinga today. It's that kind of reality that told him to quit as executive director of the Internation Microwave Power Institute when he told himself one Sunday morning in Monte Carlo that the organization he had helped found was beginning to measure itself by standards other than those which shape his life. And it's that kind of reality that makes him think it is in computers and not microwaves where his research and expertise can make the greatest impact in the years ahead. And it's that kind of reality that makes him an aggressive, uncompromising advocate of the gospel.

And, finally, maybe it's that kind of reality that keeps him in youth work, years after others have assumed it is time to pass the responsibility on to younger members. Whatever the reason, he enjoys it, even though he finds it difficult. When the Tinga family came over to Canada, the children wore the best Dutch outfits to school—short pants, cut just beneath the knees. It took them only a few classroom minutes to realize that they were the only ones who thought the new, homemade suits were in any way special. Times have changed for CR kids in Edmonton.

There isn't much difference between the CR kids and the others anymore. "There's a tremendously strong world attraction pulling at our kids from all sides," he says, "—billboards, TV, radio, all over." Materialism has an impact. "You start believing that if you *have* something—perfume or a car or whatever—you'll have happiness and security." They believe it, he says, because even their parents believe it. And those tensions make life itself a battle, not like the war, but a battle nonetheless against an enemy perhaps not as physically verifiable as a Nazi armed guard at the local post office, but present just as surely, omnipresent, and maybe more dangerous since its silent threat is aimed primarily at the soul.

"The lack of Bible knowledge is becoming a curse," he says. "Parents assume it is done by the church and school, and too often it doesn't get done." In the war with evil, a Christian unarmed with the Word is dangerously powerless, he feels. Maybe that's another reason a world authority on microwaves, a research scientist, chooses to spend hours with your kids and mine.

Whatever the reasons, he is there enjoying it, trying to help kids handle themselves in the warfare of the 80s. And maybe this year, after twenty long years of sing-alongs and zany skits and fundraisers, maybe this year those kids will finally get the professor in the lake.

7

The "Quality of Life": Shirley and Tammy Lancaster

Shirley Lancaster's story is not unusual, but it needs to be told time and time again, when pro-choice advocates discount the right to life and when professionals discuss mercykilling within the context of the "quality of life." Shirley Lancaster's daughter Tammy was born with Down's syndrome—a clinical name for what was formerly called mongolism. But Shirley Lancaster has no doubts today, five years after Tammy's death, that her daughter laughed and cried and loved for eleven of the highest quality years. What is more, Shirley knows that Tammy's special presence in the Lancaster home elevated the "quality of life" for the other three children as well.

But it's not an unusual story because we all know mothers like Shirley Lancaster, and we know their daughters or sons too. Furthermore, we know the odd paradox that characterizes the Lancaster story—that adversity carries its own rewards. Examples abound: the family was never stronger than during the depression; the church flourishes under persecution.

Shirley Lancaster wouldn't like those analogies. To her, Tammy's life represents many things, but adversity isn't one of them. Therein lies the paradox—adversity becomes blessing. And that's why we need to hear her story, over and over again.

When Tammy was born, the doctor asked Shirley if anyone in her family had slanted eyes. That was all he said, so she spent the first month of her daughter's life wondering if her fourth child had vision problems. There were no slanted eyes in her family or her husband's.

She brought Tammy in for a regular checkup after thirty days. "You know, of course, your daughter is mentally retarded," the doctor said. Of course she didn't know, and of course the revelation left her cold, unbelieving.

Another doctor came in and said, right in front of her, that he would never tell a parent such news without taking a chromosome count on the child. Shirley remembers sitting there listening, still hoping it was some crude mistake. The doctors kept bickering over what was the more humane procedure in such a case. To her mother, Tammy Lancaster was no manila file folder in some physician's office. It was her *daughter* they were discussing.

They took the count and called her back three months later. "She has Down's syndrome," they said. It was little more than a strange name to her. "She'll never walk or talk," they told her. "She'll probably be little more than a vegetable." They stood there in front of her, the child, Tammy, in her arms. They told her to try to put the child in some institution.

"They told me she was going to be nothing but problems," Shirley remembers, "but I just couldn't accept that." Shirley Lancaster reacted very rationally, the only way she says she could handle the shock. "I knew nothing about mental retardation, so I read up as much as I could." She spent hours, even weeks and months, scouring the Chicago streets looking for agencies, societies, institutions to help her learn more about Tammy, and to help Tammy herself.

Hours turned into years. She took Tammy to special programs in the city—two hours of physical therapy per day, creeping and crawling with her little daugh-

Shirley Lancaster and her son Brad:
inescapably entwined with Tammy.

ter. At four years, the "vegetable" daughter was toilet-trained and able to attend public school special education classes. "Everything she did was great to me," she remembers, "like feeding herself. People think I'm just totally patient, but I just learned to expect very little so that when she picked up something new, it was wonderful to me."

Every day mother and daughter left on city transit to different programs, and Shirley, who once knew nothing about retardation, became active in organizations for parents like herself; she became vice president of the South-Side Parents of Mentally Handicapped. Her involvement kept growing. Soon she was visiting parents who weren't as accepting of their mentally impaired kids, just talking, helping out.

Shirley Lancaster seems perfectly suited for that work. She is soft-spoken and gracious, an eager listener, but intense when she works at a point. More important, she is happy. It shows on her face. She smiles, shakes her head in near disbelief when she remembers her daughter. "She was the neatest kid when it came to eating. Much neater than the other kids." She laughs again. "Most kids with Down's syndrome are really a joy to have around—friendly and lovable. They like to hug. We just enjoyed her. My other kids learned a lot. She was like our special person, but the others treated her like they did each other and that's what was so great."

Her eyes continually address you when she speaks, but there's a discernable vagueness in them when she thinks of Tammy. "All the kids would help fold towels, and Tammy would always do a better job than her brothers and sister. I'd fuss at the others." Her face wears a mock growl. "Tammy looked at me then and said, 'Me, too, Mama, me, too.' She wanted me to fuss at her in the same way I did the others." She shakes her head. "I remember that," she says. "If I fussed at the others, I had to fuss at her too. She was a real joy.

She had something about her that just grabbed people."

In 1979, Tammy Lancaster contracted lupus, a rare disease that has symptoms like arthritis but affects organs as well as joints. At first the doctors were baffled. Tammy spent months in and out of hospitals while specialists tried to draw a diagnosis. "Rheumatoid arthritis," they told her finally, but Tammy did not seem to improve with treatment; she kept the same limp her mother had detected months before.

At Chicago's La Rabida Hospital, doctors finally diagnosed the problem. Once again, Shirley Lancaster tapped every source of information available in an effort to understand her daughter's disease.

Tammy moved in and out of hospitals as her condition worsened. Her facial features changed—"She looked like a different kid," Shirley remembers. And her joints—elbows, knees—swelled until taking a simple step was a torturous experience. The other three children would carry her to her room at night. "But she was a joy to have around," Shirley says, for the second or third time, as if you hadn't heard her say it before. "It got more and more painful though, to a point where she couldn't walk at all." The family worked on therapy at home, moving her little, misshapen limbs in an effort to keep them functional.

But it got worse. The lupus produced ulcers on her joints, and at night she'd wake up lying in blood. Shirley remembers them popping up and bleeding like big sores.

Her other children's lives became inescapably entwined with Tammy's. Every day one of them would meet her at the bus and carry her home, then stay with her for an hour or so until Shirley could get home from work.

Shirley had become a fulltime employee of the Roseland Mental Health Center, getting paid for the work she had done for years as a volunteer now that the Center had received a special grant. She remembers those painful homecomings near the end of Tammy's life. "I'd get to the door of our place, and I knew I'd have to be happy." Tammy, she knew, would be in her chair by the table, slumped over, her head down, sad. "It was like an actor readying himself to go on stage. I'd transform myself outside the door—'Hi! Hi! Hi!' I'd say, and she'd perk up some to see me there, happy. But just the thought of going in was bad. Tammy was in constant pain; I had to do it to relieve the pain."

Her son Darryl and Tammy were always very close, but when he chose to give up baseball to sit with Tammy, Shirley knew that something needed to change. Her other children had given selflessly—too much, she thought. Darryl loved baseball. Maybe, she thought, it was asking too much of them.

"So many things began falling into place. We found a perfect residential home for Tammy. When we visited there for the first time, they took her around alone, and when she came back, she was laughing." Tammy needed comprehensive care. The ulcers plagued her joints, and walking was impossible. Her face had changed her into a different child.

"It was as if we were being prepared for the end," she says, still looking back. "We were away from her for one month totally for the first time—just as though we were getting some time to get adjusted to the loss."

Unexpectedly, Tammy died of a heart attack on May 29, 1976. "She slept on away," Shirley says.

"Today we'll sit down every once in a while and talk about the things we used to do with her, how lovable she was."

First, Down's syndrome; second, lupus; third, Tammy's death. This time there was nothing for Shirley Lancaster to learn, no library bibliography to consult for an understanding of Tammy's life and death. "It got so the only way I could deal with it was to try to see it as part of a plan," she says. "That's what got me into church."

Already when they were grade-schoolers, Shirley's children had started going to an after-school program and attending Sunday school at the Pullman Christian Reformed Church. Shirley had never attended church regularly, thinking of herself as religious but feeling no need for the organized church. "After Tammy's death, the church reached out to me. I started putting things into place. The only way I could accept Tammy's death was to see the whole thing as part of a plan. It's easy to see that now. People from the church helped me to see that."

When it's hot in Chicago, it's hot like nowhere else. The sun pounds into miles of concrete, and the streets hold heat like iron. In the West Garfield neighborhood, men, women, and children come out of the old stone fortress homes for a touch of the transient lake breeze. Kids open fire hydrants in the street. Men in colorful caps and black bermuda shorts lean up against brick walls scarred by graffiti. They smoke and talk, and the Chicago streets get hot, mean.

One story up, Shirley Lancaster works in an office that can hardly be called modest. Her walls are several shades of yellow, and exposed wires lie in the corner like a ball of tangled yarn. The face of a noisy old electric fan turns from corner to corner as if on lookout. Truck noise and the whining sound of city buses storm through the open window. One story above the hot Chicago street, in an office in an old, rundown block building, Shirley Lancaster waits for a woman who has a problem with alcohol.

"She may not show up," Shirley says. "Alcoholics are often unreliable. They get to drinking . . . ."

She works for the city of Chicago, counseling alcoholics. She's chosen alcoholism because she's always wanted to know more about it. She's learning.

65

But Shirley Lancaster has already learned about the "quality of life." She's learned that, for some of us, advancement comes by inches. She's learned not to expect too much from some people, to be happy with growth that can be measured on a foot-long ruler. She's learned patience. And patience helps her to laugh, even here, upstairs in some worthless building, sitting in some eight-by-ten office cubicle, waiting for an alcoholic who may or may not show up.

It's a long view she has, a perspective, a sense of time and plot controlled by the Master Writer. Maybe it's not an unusual story at all—a mother and daughter—but it needs to be told. It's too easy for the rest of us to forget.

8

Dena Vander Wagen and Zuni

Actually, two Dutch Reformed landmarks exist in the pueblo town of Zuni, New Mexico. On one side of the street is the newly rebuilt Christian Reformed Church, its soft tan exterior blending in smoothly with the adobe homes and round outdoor ovens that line Zuni's unpaved streets. Connected to it is the Christian school, in continuous existence since 1908.

But directly across the street is the other monument, the Vander Wagen family trading store, today owned and operated by the third generation of the original CRC missionary family to the Zuni, Mr. and Mrs. Andrew Vander Wagen. Both church and store are part of the CRC legacy, whether or not we choose to claim them.

Ironically, perhaps, in 1982 there is little connection between the church/school and the complex of buildings that might be called the Vander Wagen compound. And today, Dena Vander Wagen, just a year or so past eighty years old, and her sister Billie—who, like Dena, married a son of "Grandpa Van"—are the only real links between the monuments. Dena walks through the church and school with the same comfortable familiarity she feels when reminiscing with the old Zuni butcher in the meat market of the store now run by her own nieces and nephews. In the years since Andrew Vander Wagen first stopped in the village of 1,500, most of the large Vander Wagen family have found homes in other Christian churches. Only Dena and Billie remain part of God's people called Christian Reformed.

So if you want a complete tour of the Zuni land, from the mountain gods of the native people—the windworn limestone cliffs that form enduring profiles against the wide horizon and stand like forever itself overlooking the scattered hogans of the Zuni—to the 16th-century Catholic church and graveyard; from the several Vander Wagen trading posts along the half-hour drive from Gallup to the modern Indian government hospital at Black Lake; if you want a full tour, you need Dena Vander Wagen. She will tell you how she and her husband, Ed, camped on the mountain ledges in the old days, how they hunted for deer with the Zuni, how they hiked and explored in the strange caves of the holy mountains.

In Zuni the people wave to her because she is their friend. Old men with turquoise earrings hug her as they might a sister. Old women wrapped in woolen shawls hold her like they would only touch a dear friend, and they tell her in their own language about the early summer rain dances soon to begin in the middle of the village. Young women stop their pickups in the middle of the street and step out, then embrace Dena Vander Wagen as if they were her own daughters. And Alex Seitewa, a Zuni artist now completing an impressive gallery of tribal dance portraits on the walls of the sanctuary of the reconstructed Catholic church, takes time from his work to greet her, arms extended. "When I was a boy, Dena always trusted me," he says, "even when I didn't have money to pay for food." In Zuni, Dena is loved.

For fifteen years, after her husband had died from the complications of an earlier injury, Dena Vander Wagen served up short orders in a cafe in the middle of

In Zuni,
Dena is loved.

Zuni. Today, when she remembers those years, one can feel the enthusiasm ride the constant flow of memories. "There were men from Harvard and Oxford in my cafe. People stopped in from all around the world. That was really my education," she says. But mostly it was the Zuni—her people—whom she served in that little cafe.

Today, when she walks the streets, the people tell her how well she is looking, her long, dark hair, streaked with silver, pulled back and pinned behind her head. There is an unpretentious dignity to her carriage, because she has a noticeable maternal-like strength. In the Zuni culture she is old—old and respected. She is small like the Zuni people, and in her ears and around her neck and wrist is Zuni inlay jewelry, designed by women she knows personally, women she greets on the street while they tend their adobe ovens. She is naturally quiet and unassuming, and the joy she feels when she walks on those familiar paths, the paths that surround the Vander Wagen homestead, her home, can barely be heard in the subdued reflections she makes on sixty years of life in a New Mexico Indian village.

"We lived right there, inside that very door." She points at the rickety screen at the back of the family store. She stands quietly, says nothing; but her eyes cloud with the memories that flow out of that door, as if decades hadn't interrupted. There's nothing Dutch about the back of the Vander Wagen compound today. Housewives in Hudsonville would shake their heads at the disarray; they might call it something of an unholy mess. But the Vander Wagens left a fastidious Dutch character back in Michigan. They became more Zuni than *Afscheiding.* The Zuni gave them Indian names.

Someday someone will write the Vander Wagen story, but the author will probably not be one of us. It will be a story of courage, like all missionary narratives, a story of sacrifice, of difficult life in a primitive culture. But unlike some other missionary tales, the Vander Wagen story will be a story of deep and final commitment to the area. On the road from Gallup to Zuni is a one-horse town named Vander Wagen, New Mexico. Today a third-generation Vander Wagen holds political office and represents the area. Family trading posts are sprinkled among the pinions and pines that paint the stony hills in bold green blotches. Today there are two monuments in Zuni, and it might be difficult to have to judge which monument has had the greatest effect on the culture of Zuni. Someone else will have to write the Vander Wagen story.

Dena Brink Vander Wagen came west from Allendale, Michigan, at the age of thirteen, and from the moment she arrived, she loved the high plains of New Mexico. "We never regretted coming, not at all," she says. "Rehoboth was different then, very primitive; the buildings were made of adobe bricks, and the dormitories and the chapel were a long walk away from each other, rain or shine." She came west on the train to Gallup in 1912 with her father and mother, Rev. and Mrs. J. W. Brink, and aside from a few years spent back in Grand Rapids for an education, she has spent her life on the sculptured plateaus of western New Mexico.

Her husband, Ed Vander Wagen, went "back East" for his schooling, to the Grandville Avenue Christian School, and he too returned, just about the time the Brinks initially arrived at Rehoboth to take their new position. Quite frequently in those early years, Rev. Brink would put his whole family in a wagon and make the day-long, dusty trip to Zuni, where his children could play with the only other missionary kids in the area—the Frylings and the Vander Wagens. Ed, the first white child in Zuni, worked in his father's store in 1913, having already returned from his Michigan education. A few years later, when Dena returned from her schooling and took up teaching in the Zuni

Vander Wagen, New Mexico:
a one-horse town on the road from
Gallup to Zuni.

school, Ed found a horse for her and took her out riding quite often. "We just liked each other right away," she says. They were married at Rehoboth in 1919, and they moved out to a ranch owned by Grandpa Van for their first years of married life.

Dictionaries define a missionary as "one sent to propagate the faith, doctrine, and principles of a religion among nonbelievers." In that strict dictionary sense, Dena was never a missionary. She taught Indian children, ran a store, raised three children of her own, and later cooked meals at the cafe in the middle of town. Like Grandpa Van, Dena was a missionary by avocation, someone who shared her faith in God with others through conversations that formed slowly, over dirty cafe dishes or bartered sheep pelts. Zuni may have been her own mission field, but it was and is also her home.

Today she lives in Gallup, on Hill Street, in a rectangular apartment complex and a long, narrow, three-room apartment, thirty-some miles from her home. Too far, she'll tell you. She would love to be in Zuni, but there's no place for her. She would love to walk its streets daily, to watch its seasonal litany of ceremonial dances, the same dances her husband knew as well as any Zuni boy, the same dances frowned on by generations of CRC missionaries as pagan and godless.

And, finally, she wants to die here, to be buried on a little plot of land she considers by deed her own, up above Zuni pueblo in what is called "the Vander Wagen cemetery," a plot given years ago to Grandpa Van. His grave is there today, surrounded by a white picket fence, kept neatly. Her husband is there too, and his brother Si, and a missionary child, and Gilbert Bruxvoort, and others. And there are Zunis buried there too, now that the Catholic cemetery is full.

Dena Vander Wagen says very little as she stands at her husband's grave on the cemetery knoll overlooking Zuni. She doesn't need to say much, for in her eyes is written the story of a family, a Dutch Christian Reformed family who has lived the Zuni life as long as many of our families have lived on the streets of our Orange Cities. They have roots in the gritty soil of New Mexico, where the winds blow like bullies off the high plains and over the flat land where Zuni farmers turn up the land and wait for the all-too-infrequent rains.

About an hour's hike south of Rehoboth Mission is a cove, almost a tunnel carved by wind and water out of the rock. Etched into the sides of its cliffs is a gallery of Dutch names and dates, some so old they are barely recognizable anymore. There are dozens of names, a kind of hotel registry of those who have come and gone and left their names like souvenirs of their sojourns. The Vander Wagens stayed. Their name is on the map here. Stories of Ed and Dena, their hunting conquests and their compassion, are part of Zuni legend, told by the Zuni themselves: "Many other times [Ed and Dena] killed game and gave out all the meat to their people, and the Navajo and Zuni remembered these people for their generosity" (*The Zunis: Self-Portrayal*, University of New Mexico Press).

"My father was one of those people who simply loved human beings. I guess I'm a lot like him that way," she says on her way back to Gallup, and her lips tighten as she leaves her hometown again, grudgingly. "It's hard to leave. I don't know when I'll get back again."

Sometime in the future Dena Vander Wagen anticipates two homecomings: one, a final return to her Zuni homeland; the other, even greater, with the God of the Brinks and the Vander Wagens and the Zuni.

9

John Bergman of Canada's "Banana Belt"

Long ago, some say, Lake Ontario receded from its southern shoreline and left a fertile, thumbshaped peninsula, a region playfully called Canada's "Banana Belt," the fruit capital of Ontario, maybe of the entire nation. In late summer the fruit farms show their produce in a nearly endless row of display stands, attracting customers from Toronto, the city across the lake, and from other areas—urban and rural—of the spacious province of Ontario.

But the Banana Belt has more to attract attention than its fruit stands. Southern Ontario has the escarpment, a sharp ridge of land that cuts through the flat shoreland area like some misplaced mountain ridge. Tourists from around the world flock to the escarpment; honeymooners fill the many motels. Everyone comes to see the Falls—Nigeria Falls—millions of gallons of water per second rushing off the ridges, creating an immense cloud of moisture so thick it fogs your windshield on the clearest of summer afternoons.

The Bergmans run a nursery only five miles or so from the escarpment, less than a half hour's drive from the thousands of tourists who come daily to the Falls. From the deck of his remodeled farmhouse, John Bergman can look over thirty-some miles of Lake Ontario and see Toronto's skyline etched in the horizon.

The Bergmans' land is the lakeshore; John's brother's new house stands little more than one hundred feet from the crease of land and water. The earth here is thin but rich. It spills from John's hand when he turns it in his fingers. "You can grow anything here," he says. It is sandy loam, brown and granular.

Some of the Bergmans' neighbors have vineyards. Vast improvements in varieties of grapes have been made recently, and a crop of grapes that formerly took $100 a ton now may earn a farmer five times that much. The new vineyards have inflated the price of land in the Banana Belt, but other factors have altered the way of life for residents like the Bergmans as well. Infation's effect is as notable here as anywhere in North America—that's a given today. But fifteen years ago the St. Lawrence Seaway bought up a belt of Ontario land and made plans to scoop out a canal through the narrow corner that separates Lake Erie from Lake Ontario. The canal was never built, but land prices soared.

"The price of land doubled overnight," John says. The Bergmans lease a bit more than twenty acres of Seaway land, but a few years ago, when the family business seemed too big for its acreage, the boys bought 150 acres of cheaper land near Dunville, 45 miles south, and planted the plot bushy with evergreens.

It is a family business; generally, John Bergman runs the office and handles sales. His brother Pete cultivates and sprays, and Bill, the last of nine Bergman kids, digs out the trees and bushes.

The front room of the old Bergman home is full of dust and sandy loam. Today it's the nursery's office. Johannes Bergman, like his three sons, has moved; his house, perfectly landscaped, of course, stands just an acre east. John sits in an old wooden office chair with his feet up, the desk littered with papers and colorful promotions in various shades of green.

John Bergman:
not the stereotypical salesman.

"We really don't want the business to get all that big," he says. "This is what we can handle, and we don't go crazy with a lot of people." John Bergman is a strong, outdoors type, brown-skinned, muscular. He doesn't strike you as the stereotypical salesman, although every August he peddles bushes and shrubs to retailers in Montreal and Toronto. "We enjoy it right now. My brothers and I work well together and that's worth a lot. When you get to the point that your work ceases to be enjoyable, then you'd better get out of it," he says.

But he is not blind to the fact that past financial success allows him the luxury of that perspective. Johannes Bergman, his father, left the Netherlands in 1954 with his wife and nine children, leaving behind his own tulip bulb businses. John was nine then; his oldest sister, Ada, was only 18.

It was April when they arrived. Johannes Bergman found himself on Canadian soil, down on hands and knees picking dandelions. He told himself there had to be a better way of feeding his children. Slowly a plan developed. Each of the family members who were able to make money "worked out" and paid in. Ada, Willie, Margaret—all of John's sisters—tossed their earnings into the family pot, willfully, cognizant of their part in the family's plans for financial stability in the new country.

In two years Johannes Bergman bought a house and thirteen acres of peach orchard—the beginning. The first year's fruit brought in $700; the second year's lost exactly as much. The Bergmans wanted out of peaches. Year by year the orchard went through a facelift, and five years after the purchase of the land, the thirteen acres were shorn of peaches completely. The Bergman farm had become Niagara Holland Nursery—evergreens, shrubs, fruit trees for your every landscaping need.

John started fulltime when he was twenty. "It's a beautiful business," he says. "You work with nature, you see things grow—it's great. This is the Banana Belt, man!'' Some of the salesman in him appears in his eyes, touches his voice.

The whole business seems so easy when you hear him explain it, but it is a long process. It starts with a row of potted shrubs at your local Zellers or K-Mart.

Each year, around the end of November, the Bergmans gather the whole work crew and make cuttings, 250,000 six-inch shoots from the stems of plants already salable. In January the whole gang gets together again for grafting. The cuttings are simply attached to solid root stock. In the nursery business, no one has to wait for some scientist to develop a new hybrid seed; nature itself offers the opportunity for the creation of new varieties. The Bergmans simply combine the attributes of several varieties of shrubs in concoctions they expect or know to be marketable. Graft a colorful bush or leaf onto the hearty root of some less showy relative, and you have the advantage of both—strength plus beauty. This kind of mixed marriage is the stock and trade of the Bergmans' business. John insists that if more people knew how easy grafting is, Niagara Holland Nursery would have even more competition.

By the end of May the grafted cuttings are set in straight rows, one after another, back into the Ontario soil, where they stay for a year, reaching a height of nearly three feet. The next summer they are "lined out," thinned and spread to allow for more growth and a stronger root system.

By September of the second year of growth, the whole crew pots them individually in papier-maché and shelters them in a greenhouse, out of the wind and snow. "By the next spring, they're just A-1," John says, winking.

The Bergmans aren't the only CRC family in southern Ontario who grow things in the sandy lakeshore loam. The flat land south of the escarpment and east of

Holland Niagara Nursery:
evergreens, shrubs, fruit trees for your
every landscaping need.

the Welland Canal is full of Dutch florists, all of them immigrants. Covenant CRC stands just west of the canal; you can see the roof line from the Bergmans' rented land. But seeing the church isn't like being there. Many a Sunday morning some lake barge will lumber up the canal locks, shutting off traffic between Niagara-on-the-Lake and St. Catharines. While the nursery folk and florists from the other side of the canal sit there and wait in their Sunday best, the ship struggles up the locks and the rest of the church waits.

The church is like a family that way, waiting for everyone to show up. And that kind of family identity is an attribute John Bergman recalls about the church during those early years in the 50s. "The church gave us a sense of belonging, a real sense of unity that we needed as immigrants." There was never a question about the church in Bergman family discussions. Attendance was simply expected. But the kids wouldn't have thought of skipping, really, not church and not Young Peoples. "We always did things in a church context. Our friends were all there. We looked forward to it. Going to church was our time for socializing." That's the way he remembers it.

Oddly, paradoxically perhaps, it's this same family character that John Bergman recognizes as inhibiting today's church, the family church in which he grew up, the old church in the new land. "Our church is still a Dutch church, and we have to get away from that. That's our fault; we stuck close together. And now, after twenty-five years, it's not so easy to shed that Dutch image," he says.

It's a perplexing thing, trying to reform the church by rejecting one of its greatest attributes. But John Bergman knows it will happen. "Our kids aren't Dutch anymore. They're Canadians. We are just now trying to get out of the old insulated world. But it's not easy."

When John Bergman walks through his tree plots, the silver maples and the red maples, he reaches out and touches the saplings, pulls their leaves through his open hand as if he were petting them, as if they felt him there next to them. "You know," he says, "we're not like some others. We've had all kinds working here for us—Catholics, United Church, even atheists, most everything. They talk about church in a different way than we do. We're not like some others at all. You get to thinking that it doesn't mean the same thing to them as it does to us—the church, their faith. Our whole life centers around the church." Instinctively, he reaches down and jerks a weed out of a tree plot.

John Bergman sees this difference as a barrier to attracting new people into the church—as much of a barrier as a thick brogue or a biannual trip back home to Holland. "Most people don't look at the church like we do," he says again.

In the greenhouse, grafting is a simple procedure: you have two plants, two attributes, and you simply fuse them together, lock up the graft with a rubber band, and bury the joint in warm, moist soil. In less than a decade you have a beautiful shrub with a powerful root system.

Would that grafting were so easily accomplished in the church.

10

Bev Den Bleyker:
Growing Up in Graafschap

If you are driving south on M-31 out of Holland, all you'll see of Graafschap is the church steeple poking out of the elms, like some sleepy memory of an old, precious way of life. But if nostalgia pulls at you like gravity, and you turn back and take a couple of winding roads, before you know it you'll be right in the middle of Graafschap, a sweet, old one-church town.

It's a blessing to stand in front of the old white church, to stand there and think that the one long beam spanning the entire church was set in place more than 120 years ago by Dutch and German hands, hands of people in whose ancestral shadow we live and worship. You can almost hear them setting it yet; and, if you listen closely, you can hear the old psalms, and you can see the black hats, the beards, and the horse barns over there beyond the sanctuary. In a sense, we were all born in towns like Graafschap.

Bev Den Bleyker lives in Graafschap. She was baptized in the old white church with the historic beam, and she and her husband, Vern, were married there. For much of her life she has lived on the same block, in the old family home near the softball field. Vern grew up next door. He used to give her rides on his big, blue-and-white Cushman scooter. They dated throughout high school, the girl and the boy next door. "It seems like I knew him his whole life," she says. They grew up together, not a ground-rule double from the church, and they rode the same bus to Holland Christian School —the bus Vern's dad always drove.

You're never alone in a small town, a one-church town like Graafschap. There are always aunts and grandpas, and neighbors who are probably more "family" than the renegade uncle who up and moved to East Lansing. Small towns make growing up as easy as growing up can be. Small towns smile when their own kids date each other; they cry when the same kids kneel at the front of the church, when the first wedded kiss lingers a couple heartbeats too long.

Tradition is like an interstate highway, all its entrances and exits clearly marked by overhead signs with arrows that point your way to a specified destination. Traveling is easy on an interstate, sometimes too easy. Maybe that's why Vern and Bev's courtship moved along on obscure country roads for five, almost six years. "I always knew I would marry him," she says, "but there were times when I couldn't live with him and I couldn't live without him." On again, off again, through summers of softball games. When Vern would see the same guy's car too often next door at Bev's, he'd start it up again and spend some time over there himself. Off and on. Graafschap watched.

In October 1965, just back from basic training with a local reserve unit, Vern made big plans; he and Bev talked of marriage, she just two years out of Holland Christian High. But then in December, he panicked. "I'm not ready," he told Bev one night while parked in her driveway. "I was hurt," she says. "We had been going together for five years."

Off and on. Off and on. Engaged in February 1966, broken off again in March of the same year. This time it was Bev who broke it, more sure of her own devotion than she was of his. She went to Denver, moved away from the boy next door. "I kept seeing him," she says, "because he lived right there." She left directions that no address be given. But she left her address somewhere in Graafschap, and there are not many secrets in small towns.

Ah, but love will out! Vern found Bev's address and called her landlord. Bev had no phone; she didn't want to be reached by the boy next door. But he called her at midnight, said he wanted her back. "He was persuasive," she admits with a glorious, small-town smile. "But I told him I would have to pray about it."

Long into the night Bev and her roommate talked. And later, when she couldn't sleep, she knelt at her bedside. It was near morning. The doorbell rang while she was on her knees, and from her bedroom window she saw him standing outside the door in a yellow shirt and tan pants. (Some images one never forgets.) "Ja, ja," the old men of Graafschap would say, "the Lord works in mysterious ways." And sometimes he uses jet travel. It's a good Graafschap story; you can bet it was told over coffee, even after church.

Something over four years later, Mr. and Mrs. Vern Den Bleyker had a quiverful—three kids. "People would ask me how I could put up with it—three little ones in such a short time," she remembers. "Sometimes I felt that I couldn't." She wouldn't have admitted it, of course. Generally, small towns have very clear standards for motherhood.

"I was physically and emotionally drained," she says. But no one knew because, while there may be no secrets in small towns, some things are much better left unsaid. "I guess at the time I felt that all I had was God; he gave me the strength I needed. It was something that happened inside of me."

A long tradition, a close family, the Christian school, an old white church with an ancient beam—these things can guide us efficiently, but there comes a time when one needs to live on something other than bor-

Bev Genzink Den Bleyker:
a glorious, small-town smile.

rowed breath. For Bev and Vern Den Bleyker, personal commitment had been somehow neglected. She knew this when her God pulled her out of her depression. In a small town full of Christian Reformed people, in a culture brimming with ethno-religious traditions, Vern and Bev discovered that the covenant God of the old Graafschap church was also the sovereign Lord of their own lives, their kids, their hurts, their joys. Some would even call what they felt a "conversion."

Their devotions became more personal as their commitment grew. Then, five years of growth later, a friend challenged them. He had been to Alaska, to a Christian training school for Indians and Eskimos. When he told them about the place, they began to wonder about the direction of their own lives. "Maybe you ought to think about going," the friend told them. "Pray about it." But they lived in the family house in Graafschap, Vern had recently bought his own business, the kids were all enrolled in Christian school, and every Sunday they walked to the old white church. They were living a comfortable Graafschap life.

They prayed together as a family. They applied and were accepted for a position at the Alaskan school. "It's amazing how things that seemed important—the business, for example—suddenly seemed unimportant," she remembers. Vern and Bev and their four children left the family home in town for a wilderness boarding school in the Alaskan Rockies, one hundred miles from a grocery store.

"If you had asked me what I thought of the church before we went to Alaska, my answer would have been different than today," she admits, sitting back in the shadow of the old church, back home in Graafschap again. Bev and Vern have been to the mountain top. It took Eskimo kids, an environment stripped of the media, and a family of believers in frontier Alaska. Today Bev says that working at the training school gave both of them the greatest fulfillment of their lives. It was confrontation that did it, the necessity of open, verbalized commitment—testimonies on a daily basis. "We often rely on the church and the school to give spiritual training," she says, "but we couldn't do that at Victory High School." The Den Bleykers were forced into a kind of openness and commitment that too often makes little Dutch towns and big CR churches somewhat uneasy.

"I'm really proud of the Graafschap church," she admits, but the Alaskan experience changed her perspective. "We're missing the boat sometimes, I think. Growing up here, we learned the scriptural foundations of academic subjects. But commitment was never pulled out of me. I was never in a situation where I had to say what all of this meant to me personally. Even profession of faith for me was merely a graduation from catechism. We went with maybe fifteen or twenty of us."

Bev Genzink Den Bleyker has changed. The Spirit, she'll tell you, is more obviously present in the life of the family today. The God of Graafschap church has entered their lives in a way they hadn't experienced before. Close to forty, Vern is enrolled at Reformed Bible College now; he plans to be a teacher. Bev will audit some classes this term. The Alaskan experience pulled them out of a CRC cubicle and forced them to defend the beliefs they grew up with—infant baptism, for example. Both Bev and Vern want to know not only what they believe, but why. That may sound odd, the Den Bleykers both growing up in a birthplace of the CRC.

Finally, the Alaskan experience has liberated her, enabled her to see things she hadn't seen before, even the old church. "I love my heritage and my background," she says. "I'm not sure I would see my heritage in the same way I do today if we hadn't gone to Alaska."

Our Graafschaps deserve honor. Tradition grants

stability and roots. Tradition shows us who we have been and points us where we might go.

But Bev Den Bleyker listens to the morning church bells every Sunday, and she knows, today, that each of our old, white Graafschap churches must be a whole lot more than just another stop on some Tulip Time tour.

The church cannot stand on the strength of one wooden beam, no matter how ancient or how honorable.

11

Dr. Condon Vander Ark, Cardiologist

Dominie Seine Bolks deserves a biography. In the late decades of the 19th century, this man worked in new immigrant communities from Michigan to Illinois to Wisconsin to Iowa, ministering to the spiritual needs of the strangers on American soil. But, in addition, Bolks, likely one of the only educated persons in many of these hamlets, ministered to physical needs as well. By necessity, perhaps, Bolks became a rural medical practitioner, delivering dozens of Wytzes and Geertjes into the sheltered world of an ambitious generation of immigrants devoted, like Bolks himself, to the establishment of a new and permanent home.

Today, a century later, Dr. Condon Vander Ark, acting head of cardiology at the University of Wisconsin Medical School in Madison, is a kind of heir to the ancestral legacy of Seine Bolks; and in contrast, Vander Ark's work illustrates the vast change God's time has wrought in the Reformed community. Vander Ark, an academic physician, is a specialist, a cardiologist, someone whose expertise has focused exclusively on the diagnosis and medical management of cardiovascular diseases. As such, he deals primarily with referred patients—patients, for instance, whose own doctors, recognizing something unusual or peculiar in their heart functions, have sent them along to someone whose research and practice is devoted entirely to heart problems. Under the care of Vander Ark, the patients and their doctors expect that the most modern technology will be used in diagnosis and treatment.

Vander Ark is in academic medicine—teaching, research, and high-level clinical practice. It is incumbent upon him to keep up with everything—the most advanced technological apparatus, the most recent scientific achievement—everything occurring in a field of medicine where textbooks are printed in paperback because the information they hold becomes so quickly out-of-date—obsolete almost annually.

The University of Wisconsin Hospital is a new, modern modular castle that spreads out like an architectural fantasy over acres of rolling terrain, overlooking Madison's Lake Mendota and just across the street from the only church ever designed by Frank Lloyd Wright. The hospital is a complex creation of short corridors and infields, of individual patient rooms and tiny office spaces, and it offers an awesome challenge to anyone who is unacquainted with its intricate floor plan.

Wright himself would have liked the place, for if the hospital's form doesn't exactly follow its function, it certainly mirrors the complexity of its business. Besides providing quality patient care, the University Hospital exists as a classroom and a laboratory—a training ground for specialists in many areas of medicine: psychosomatic medicine, gastroenterology, nephrology, hematology, rheumatology, and a host of other "ologies" even more foreign to the ears of those of us who have been blessed by nothing worse than a pesky cough and runny nose. Such specialization requires sophisticated technology whose operation is even more incredible than its price tag. Such technology requires expertise that, to a layperson, seems many times more formidable than finding your way around the University Hospital.

91

Dr. Condon Vander Ark:
wishing sometimes he were a veterinarian.

Dr. Vander Ark's specialty, cardiology, lies under the rubric of internal medicine. "Cardiology," he says, "is unique from the other subspecialties of medicine, in the sense that cardiology has become a very technological subspecialty. We use a lot of diagnostic procedures and tests that are rather nontraditional in medicine." Echo-cardiography, for example, is the use of ultrasound to bounce sound waves off the heart walls and valves in the chest and return them to an elaborate machine that videotapes heart motion. This technique allows the cardiologist to visualize and measure the movements of the heart and thereby determine the anatomic and functional state of the heart.

Such technology would, of course, be beyond the ken of Dominie Bolks. Such technology is far beyond the ken of most of us, reared even as we were during the age of technology. Such unimaginable sophistication characterizes Vander Ark's practice. It is the science of medicine.

To many, *science* connotes the sterile, the antiseptic, the clinical, something as lifeless and uncompromising as hard, cold fact. But the machinery of cardiology does not obfuscate the humanness of Vander Ark's calling. While the student labs—replicas of the operating rooms—are stocked with dogs and pigs, Vander Ark's machinery is aimed primarily at the human heart —the heart of a grandmother, a father, or even a child.

And today it's Christmas at the hospital. The angling corridors are rich with the smell of a potluck lunch, the antiseptic hidden, today at least, beneath the aromas of pasta and chili and chicken gumbo. But the work goes on, and somewhere an old man, his gray, hairless body swathed in hospital linens, has been through a percutaneous transluminal angioplasty, an incredibly intricate procedure in which the physician pokes a tiny balloon through the patient's artery until it reaches a troublesome vessel too dangerously close to closing. When the balloon is inflated, this artery expands

93

enough to allow a healthy flow of blood and oxygen. But today the operation, initially successful, has failed due to bleeding in the artery wall. Now, unfortunately, the man on the cart is wheeled off to surgery, where he will undergo a coronary bypass or two, the alternative to the balloon dilatation.

There's sadness in the face of the attending cardiologist who explains this to Vander Ark, not only because this time the new technology has not been the answer, but also because the man on the cart, strung with tubes and monitors, will now face an extended hospital stay. If the new treatment had been effective, he could have joined his wife and their grandchildren for Christmas. The IV bottle hooks the tinsel and rips it down from the doorway as the nurses rush him off to a surgery everyone—family, friends, doctors, and he himself—wished, hoped, prayed he could have missed.

Underneath the balloons, the sound waves, and the computer printouts is the Hippocratic Oath and the people whose emotions, minds, and souls the medical profession serves, laypeople befuddled by the maze of technological medicine. Vander Ark insists that over-expectation may be the most difficult hurdle to overcome in treating human beings. It's not that difficult to understand why overexpectation occurs frequently in a society where the advancements of science long ago passed the understanding of those not directly involved. For we make the assumption that a doctor's ability both to know the exact nature of our malady and to treat that problem is directly related to the amount of hardware at her or his disposal. And we laypeople are most distrustful when a doctor, armed with the most sophisticated machinery, must finally admit that one plus two does not always equal three. "After all, we can put people on the moon, why can't we...?" We have heard the line so often we believe it, even if we call it an unexamined analogy.

But cardiology does not always have concrete

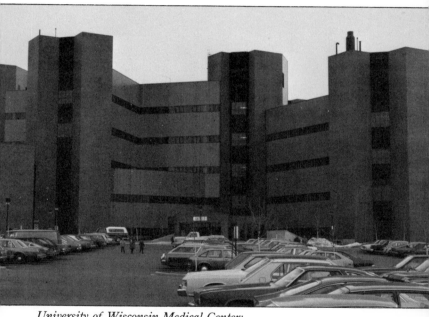

University of Wisconsin Medical Center:
an architectural fantasy.

answers to the ultimate questions people have. Unlike the cancer patient whose disease has reached the terminal phase and has, therefore, a seemingly relentless course, the heart patient, according to Vander Ark, "lives with the expectation that tomorrow things will be no worse and maybe will be better than today. Then, suddenly, the patient is gone." Thus the human dimension intrudes in a scientific world. Thus, Vander Ark must practice the art, as well as the science, of medicine.

To a doctor/scientist, working with human beings can be rewarding but frustrating. "Sometimes I wish I were a veterinarian," he says, "because, if I would tell a farmer that his hogs needed injections of something every day for two weeks, I could probably count on it being done. With humans it's another story." He looks around as if disturbed, then smiles. "I could show you patients who've had heart surgery who are right this minute sitting in some waiting room somewhere smoking a cigarette." Those of us who have lost faith in medicine might check the number of old pills left in our bathroom cabinets and consider our doctors' difficulties.

It would be difficult not to trust Dr. Condon Vander Ark. He is a tall man; his hair and Vandyke beard are streaked with silver. He strikes you as the kind of man who might be doing TV commercials for, say, Accutron watches—he casts that kind of handsome, knowledgeable appearance. He speaks with the precision one would expect from a man whose life is a daily agenda of significant decisions, whose mind, like the library in his office, is stacked with information and data. His desk is full of memos and minutes of meetings and scratch pads from pharmaceutical companies; his office is small, reflecting the career choice for academic medicine, a choice he made after a two-year army stint in the early 60s—he was drafted at 27, already the father of three and a recent graduate of the University of Michigan Medical School.

His entire personal history—a Grand Rapids boy, Baxter and Sylvan and Oakdale Christian Schools, Central Christian High, Calvin College—is a tribute to his own personal dedication, as well as to the tradition of people like Seine Bolks. He says he never knew a doctor when he was growing up and hadn't the foggiest notion of what being a doctor was all about. Besides, he says, all the other Vander Arks were teachers, a fact which, he admits, may have had something to do with his eventual decision to opt for academic medicine.

There's a huge brown book in Vander Ark's office, in size and weight roughly equivalent to the old *Staten Bijbel* Dominie Bolks himself may have owned. It's a huge thing, a scary thing, titled simply *Heart Disease.* It probably weighs over ten pounds. There's a lot of truth in its 2,000 pages, packed with charts, diagrams, photos, and entire sections full of data—the accumulation of decades of research on the human heart. But some of it will be dated tomorrow, if not yet this afternoon.

"Science and secular philosophy don't provide honest and satisfactory answers to many fundamental questions," Vander Ark says. "Christ fills in these gaps, and Christianity does provide honest answers. Christ gives a sense of purpose to life, a meaning, a consistent way of seeing oneself in relation to the world he has made. And I know that because he tells me that it's true—it's the gift of faith. I treasure the way a friend of mine puts it: 'That man is at peace whose God is sovereign.' "

Dominie Bolks would have smiled at that confession even if truth, to him, seemed a whole world more simple.

12

Randalyn Munsey of Southern California

Unlike the French, we have no official watchdogs over the state of our language or its mechanics. Innovations occur, it seems, by consensus. So when someone, somewhere, decided that the *southern* of Southern California should begin with a capital *S,* few English language users disagreed, or so it would appear. We don't capitalize northwestern Iowa or western Michigan or southern Ontario, much as our own provincial pride might desire it. Only Southern California merits such lavish salutation.

And we all know why. If you tell someone you live in southern Wisconsin, you would probably be asked how far that is from Milwaukee. Tell someone you're from Southern California and immediate pictures appear. The connotations of the phrase roll out in rapid succession like the frothing waves off Laguna Beach.

Southern California is Hollywood, MGM, Paramount, all the stars from *National Enquirer.* Southern California is Venice, nude beaches, hot tubs, cocaine—glorified decadence. Southern California is suntans, palm trees, oranges, retirement gardens—American paradise. Southern California is a perpetual gilded age—Rolls Royce Silver Shadows, hillside mansions, Disneyland, the Crystal Cathedral. Roller skating, hula hoops, waterbeds, rock music—trace any of a dozen cultural phenomena to their origins and you'll find the base of the rainbow in Southern California—with a capital *S*.

The Christian Reformed Church came to Southern California because Dutch immigrants—some from Holland and some from the dust-blown midwestern farm towns—wanted *their* church with them in the area once known as "Dairy Valley." First CRC of Bellflower mushroomed from 30 or 40 families to 350 in the early years, and the original church begat daughters in Ontario and later in Chino, the dairy farmers trucking their herds further and further away from what was rapidly becoming a mega-city.

Calvary CRC is a daughter of First Bellflower—probably a granddaughter or more, if we are plotting a family tree. It stands in line with office and apartment complexes and fast-food chains on Chino's Walnut Avenue, one of thousands of carbon-copy Southern Cal thoroughfares. Not a dairy in sight; a reminder that Southern California may like milk, but it doesn't appreciate cows. You will probably find some family names from First Bellflower if you check Calvary's church directory, but its calling and identity as a church differ from the identity sought by those early depression immigrants. Calvary CRC does more than preserve and feed a congregation that is already a family; it also reaches out into the housing developments that have grown on what was once dairy land. It reaches for people like Randalyn Munsey.

Randalyn Munsey is a typical Californian, if there is such a person. If Southern California means youth and health and beauty, then Randi Munsey, mother of four, second-generation Californian, fits the definition. Her dark hair and tan give her that fit sunbelt look, something appropriate for a TV commercial. She has worked at two favorite California jobs: as a waitress at the Disneyland Blue Bayou Restaurant and as a real

Randalyn Munsey:
tuning to the right station.

estate escrow officer. She is a fine American mix of ethnic flavors, and her family roots, like those of so many of her friends, run back east. In a metropolitan area built on the convenience of the automobile, she has moved frequently—Long Beach, Placentia, Anaheim, Chino. And, like too many other Californians, Randi has lived with brokenness: her real father and mother were divorced when she was a year old, and her stepfather and mother were divorced when she was twelve.

For four years she lived about a block from Calvary CRC in Chino, but it was an invitation from a family psychologist that pulled her through the big front doors one Sunday morning. "It didn't take more than a couple of weeks before I realized that this was where I wanted to be," she says today, two years after that first Sunday she and her mother took the five-minute walk to church. And she speaks highly of her new family today: "They're just full of love. Each time we came, different people made us feel at home."

Devotional literature is filled with stories of miraculous conversions on death beds, on surgical tables, in foxholes. Randi Munsey's conversion is not nearly so dramatic, but it is nonetheless miraculous. For her it was a gradual process toward commitment and fulfillment. It may sound strange to say it, but Calvary CRC was simply in the right place at the right time—which is a rather unfancy way of defining providence.

"Jesus Christ is my Savior," she admits today. The phrase is an old one, maybe even trite in an era when it may be fashionable to be part of American evangelicalism. But Randi's own spiritual odyssey turns the phrase in a new direction, filling a void she felt for years but could not define before coming to Calvary.

Three generations past and a thousand miles east, Randi Munsey's maternal great-grandparents joined company with the new Christian Science Church, becoming devout members. Randi's grandmother raised her mother without doctors, but in the passing of the generations, the ardor diminished, until Randi and her brother and sister were sent, alone, to Sunday school at the Christian Science Church. Despite the weakness of her affiliation, she knew only the Christian Science faith; and several of its tenets, no matter how weakly rooted, remained with her. "Jesus Christ was the Healer," she says, "a very great healer, but not the Savior."

"I always believed in God," she says. "And there's no sin or hell in a Christian Science church, so I'm going along thinking I'm just perfect—I'm made in God's likeness and he's perfect."

But her grandmother's glaucoma made clear the weakness of the church she was reared in. In good Christian Science fashion, the practitioner, not the doctor, was called in to minister to the woman. When the glaucoma persisted, even worsened, Randi heard the practitioner blame her grandmother, indict the old woman for her lack of faith. She knew something was wrong. Once old enough to decide on her own, Randi never returned to the church her great-grandparents had helped form.

But it took a child or two, and an illness, and her mother's nervous breakdown—and finally that strange, undefined, ever-gnawing emptiness to bring her completely to God through his Son. Her children growing, she was prompted to look for fellowship with other mothers, and she found it, temporarily, in Christian Womens Club, an organization designed for mothers like Randi Munsey, largely unchurched women searching for answers to questions they lack the experience or background to ask. The monthly meetings and Bible studies were a beginning, a significant but limited start.

Still later, a bout with strep led to a heart irregularity that her own fears turned into a threat. Tired, afraid, her weakness sharpened by the old sense of emptiness, she asked herself ultimate questions: What if she were to die? For what purpose had she lived?

Ironically, she stopped going to Christian Womens Club when the need for fulfillment, for faith, was never greater. Yet, perceptibly, it kept growing, this desire to know more, to find the kind of rest and support and strength she failed to locate within herself. A car accident, drug treatment, and resulting mental strain hit her mother and threatened to take both of them down to complete collapse.

Her mother sought help at the San Antonio Mental Health Unit, the Voorman Clinic, a family counseling center created by CRC psychologists. Arlo Siegersma, a psychologist, sensing that omnipresent emptiness, suggested that both of them—mother and daughter together—try the Calvary CRC, just up the block, the one they had passed for years on their way to the supermarket.

It was as if she had had the radio on for a lifetime but never had tuned to the right station. She became involved in Calvary's Coffee Break Bible Study almost immediately, and she realized that the effect of studying God's Word with other women, then worshiping with them on Sunday, brought a more sustaining strength than Christian Womens Club could give. "You can sense the difference between Bible Coffee and Christian Womens," she says. "I really needed Christian Womens at one time, but I need Bible Coffee's structure and study today."

Pastor Al Mulder told Randi and her mother that they shouldn't make any unstudied commitments. He told them to try other churches before joining Calvary. "But I could tell this was a church of Christ. The Bible is the main theme, and the sermons guide you in your daily life. I need to grow, and you can't help but grow when you're around a group of people who generate so much love, and they do—boy, they do."

Her mother, she, her three children—all were baptized

together, March 9, 1980. "I felt the strength right away because I was ready," she says. Her enthusiasm is infectious, and apparently there is little immunity, at least not among her friends and neighbors. She's personally guided several others—women and children and entire families—to Bible Coffees and Calvary CRC, convinced that what is offered there is the Bread of Life.

But it has not all been California sunshine. Her husband, Tom, is not, has never been, a believer. She admits her initial error in working with him, hammering him with faith, hanging religion in front of him like a carrot before an animal. "Pastor Mulder told me 1 Peter 3 was my guide," she says, and as a result her strategy changed, diminished in sheer force, perhaps, but not in hope or design. Slowly, things have happened. When they brought baby Curt forward to be baptized, Tom held him, standing in front of the entire congregation. She remembers that moment and treasures it; there is love and hope in her sunshine smile.

Maybe she has learned from her own long trek. She has learned that one must be ready for commitment, that one isn't saved by a church—no matter how loving—or by an individual—no matter how saintly. She has learned that all of God's children are saved by grace alone. "In God's time," she tells herself today, "not mine."

Come to think of it, that's a lesson those original Dutch patriarchs, grounded as they were in the Heidelberger, staunch old pillars, would have found more glorious than even the grandest ocean sunset, more rich than the milk of the finest herd of Holsteins.

13

The Leader Cafe, Paul and Anita Schelhaas, Proprietors

Last week Marshall McLuhan—the global village man, the media prophet who foretold the death of print in strange, pictorial paperbacks that ironically became required reading—that Marshall MuLuhan died.

In Edgerton, Minnesota's Leader Cafe, no one mourned his death; few, perhaps, had even noted his presence. None of the men in jean jackets and hooded sweatshirts gave a hill of beans for Marshall McLuhan because McLuhan's own personal global village does not extend to many of the flat, frame villages of what Hamlin Garland called America's "Middle Border"—at least not as yet. In fact, it probably does not extend into any area where the business of life is accomplished only with the graces of a fickle mother nature, those places where the hand of God can be as harsh as an August hailstorm or as loving as a midsummer shower.

This Saturday morning, as usual, weather is the main topic over hot coffee—weather and that other determiner, the markets, both today's and those they call the "futures." It would be terribly naive, even romantic, to assume that Edgertons can still exist independent from the real global village. The men who sit in groups and sip coffee here every morning know full well that there are other forces far beyond their control, forces that determine, like it or not, their own standard of living for the next calendar year, and the next and the next. Somebody, after all, sets prices for the pork and beef and corn and soybeans they produce. The thing is, they didn't need a Marshall McLuhan to tell them this.

Edgerton felt the global village already in the 30s, and many of its residents remember firsthand the Dust Bowl and the bank collapse. In fact, more than a few of today's residents picked up what they could salvage from South Dakota and headed here, hoping this little village just above the lip of Minnesota's Blue Mounds could be another shot at the good life in a broad new country.

So the coffee sippers hit some other topics, too, as the cafe slowly fills one January morning—Iran, what Reagan will do about the hostages, the Vikings, the playoffs—and the visored caps with COOP or AMOCO or MACK nod together agreeably. By eight-thirty the counter stools are full, a square table by the wall is totally surrounded, and the men keep coming, starting more tables toward the front of the cafe. Some leave, but others arrive. By nine, some have even returned. No one orders from menus, and everyone helps himself to hot coffee steaming away on hot plates up at the cash register. Some men have ten-year standing orders —cake and egg, or toast, or two eggs easy over— orders that appear as if out of nowhere not ten minutes after they ring the bells hanging from the front. It's the honor system here. Paul Schelhaas, the manager, doesn't make any change at all until noon. The men help themselves from a cigar box that, by ten, looks like a Sunday school collection plate.

The Leader's specialty is "pigs"—sausage baked in bread dough—and they appear soon after eight. By nine the rolls from Edgerton's bakery sit right up front by the coffee in sinfully sweet straight rows. By ten the place is full.

Anita and Paul Schelhaas:
"at the end of the world"?

"Did you hear about Ben Vander Stoep? Walks into the post office the other day, early in the morning, sees a man from the back, thinks it's Iky Walhof, goes up to him like he always does, you know, and gives him a punch right on the rear. Man turns around and it's the preacher from First Reformed."

They pour second cups themselves.

"Fred Wallenburg's out back of his place last week—ya' hear this one? So he sees a calf moving out of the pen. Picks up a stone and wings it over there. Just then the calf—450 pounds almost—looks up at him, and the stone plunks him solid right between the eyes. Knocks the calf cold dead right there on the spot."

There's a rack up behind the counter, and it's full of counter slips, probably thirty or forty separate nails for the regulars at the Leader Cafe. They pay monthly sometimes.

"That Augie Stempvoort is next to crazy, you know? Tuesday morning Bill Wykstra comes in here about ten—he always helps out down at the funeral home, you know—and Augie's sitting right here at the corner stool. Wykstra pours himself a cup, and Augie says just off the top of his head, you know, he says, 'You got another watch for sale this morning, Bill?'"

In some ways, the operation of the Leader Cafe is more of a public service than anything else. From six till eleven, there might be a hundred townfolk and farmers hunched over their cups, but Paul Schelhaas isn't busy building condominiums with the profits he takes in. "I'm a nickel-and-dime business in a dollar world," he says, seated on the end of the right-angled counter. His father was a local businessman himself— Clover Farm Grocery, then Huisken's Market—and a board member of the schools Paul attended, the local Christian schools. A graduate of Dordt College in 1970, Paul, like so many others, taught school because, well, because it was almost expected of a college graduate then. He spent three years at Western Christian in Hull, Iowa. That was enough.

His father's death in 1974 brought him back to Edgerton and his wife, Anita Nawyn, a native of New Jersey, to rural midwestern housewifery, a fairly sharp cultural shift. "At first I thought I was at the end of the world," she says, but today, six years later, the mother of three boys, Anita says she loves it here on the Plains —the skies, the stars, the incredible quiet, and the freedom, being able to walk freely at night. "I used to be numb to the noise of the city, but today I get nervous when we go back, and I don't like it—the sirens, the traffic, the jets." Otherwise, the way of life seems somewhat similar in both places. In both worlds, she says, the Christian Reformed people exist in a kind of enclosed group, a group within the outside world.

But she likes her church in Edgerton, even if she sometimes feels discriminated against by not being allowed a vote in church matters. "I get angry when I realize I don't have a say, but, as I get older, I realize I have a voice in a lot of other things—service jobs, helping the needy, other things," she says, her Jersey accent still drawing her vowels out past the accepted limits of Midwest pronunciation. "I would just like to have a vote sometimes," she says. "Paul and I don't always agree on everything."

She has found her church and community to be a great comfort. "When our son Nathan was a baby, I couldn't believe the way people treated us—how loving and caring they were." Her face is youthful and clear and pretty. "And I'm learning so much all the time about the Bible, taking it book by book; I never really did that before." She speaks highly of her friends and her study group. "We're learning, we're feeling, we're helping each other. I wouldn't have time for any more involvement than I already have." She says she favors women as deacons, but she fears a church run by women. "I've seen what can happen out East, in other

The Leader Cafe:
"a nickel-and-dime business
in a dollar world."

churches," she says. "The church becomes mostly women."

Paul has some fears for the church too, but he insists that the strength of the Christian Reformed Church can overcome them. "The preaching of the Word," he says, "is still most important to the life of our church. And the catechism. We need it, we need to hear it preached." Why? "Because it outlines everything we believe. It's most important."

Preaching, and its centrality to our way of life, often contributes to a situation that he deplores, however. "Sometimes I think that the ministers have too much power in the church, from day-to-day things to synod," he says. But he is very much aware that abdication of responsibility by laypeople often leads to that kind of "dominocracy." And he acknowledges readily that the preacher and his ability to preach to the needs of the congregation is often the most significant determiner of a healthy and energetic church life.

"I like to see preachers in the cafe," he says, a characteristic naughty smile twitching a corner of his lips, "not because I'm interested in taking their quarters, but because they need to be a part of the community. Maybe that's important to preaching; at least I think it is."

By eleven, Anita subs for Paul and the coffee shop serves up lunch from a narrow little kitchen in the corner. The clientele changes; work crews building the new rural water system or the new implement garage stop in for a hot meal, an inexpensive hot meal with real home cooking—mashed potatoes and gravy, green beans, coleslaw, hot beef.

There's a handpainted rectangular sign on the wall of the Leader Cafe that says, "Will the last one up in Edgerton please remember to turn out the lights?" It came from Anita's parents in New Jersey, a gift for the Schelhaas family enterprise. "They really like it here," Anita says of her parents. "The men think the sign is

111

great," Paul says, his hand on the coffee pot. "Want me to warm it up some?"

Marshall McLuhan is dead. In the Leader Cafe, they're still talking about the weather, the Vikings, and the futures.

14

Four CRC Politicians

Maybe the reason more of us don't go into politics is the capitol buildings. They stand in the middle of our cities like strange monuments to Greek gods—many of them, anyway. Surrounded by heroic-looking statues, mottos chiseled in marble, elegant fountains, and perfectly manicured lawns, their golden domes dominate the skylines of capital cities or lie in a nest of stone and concrete, the complex of government buildings that house courts, agencies, and bureaucracies beyond tally.

You might think there's more hardwood in the Iowa state capitol building itself than in the entire state, and it would probably take a week to note all the murals, historical artifacts, Corinthian columns, and incredible extravagance of a nearly century-old building. Nothing like it could be built today, of course; the time and artistry needed to create such a palace is beyond the ways and means of any committee. It intimidates, especially if you were born on the flat cornfields of Iowa, especially if you remember painting barns or forking hay or walking endless rows of soybeans with a short hoe in your right hand.

The Iowa state capitol buildings themselves may intimidate people who are more at home with concrete silos and farrowing houses, but you can't tell it in the Iowa legislature. Four Christian Reformed Church members work in the place: two Democrats, Senator Bass Van Gilst of Oskaloosa and Representative Bill Dieleman of Pella; and two Republicans, Senator Richard Vande Hoef of Ocheyedan and Representative Harold Van Maanen of Oskaloosa. All four share the farm heritage; Van Gilst, Van Maanen, and Vande Hoef are still farmers by profession. And they have held one additional office in common—all have been elders in their local churches.

Senator Vande Hoef was awed by the capitol when, in January 1981, he walked up the long flights of steps to the Senate chamber and picked out his seat in the semicircle of desks and papers and microphones facing that of the President of the Senate. But he was awed even more by the responsibility of an office granted him by the voters of his district, an office that only two years before he would never have guessed he would be filling.

Vande Hoef is a powerfully built man with massive farmer's hands. His dark hair is streaked with silver; his face is thin and almost leathery from long hours in the field. Most of his life has not been spent behind a desk.

Politics is new to Vande Hoef. Going out on the campaign trail and singing his own praises were new to him—and somewhat repulsive. Today, four months into his first term, the sharp sting of political debate is new to him. "At times it's more angry and intense than I expected," he says.

The decision to run was no easy step for him to take. In November 1979, at a local Republican meeting, Vande Hoef was encouraged, publicly, to seek the office of a retiring friend. "I spent six weeks praying about it with friends and family and the pastor," he says, "because I believe the office should seek the individual, not the other way around." His weaknesses, he says, appeared during that time of decision-making, and when he opted to run, he trusted God to help him, especially in those areas.

"Too often we're unwilling to get involved," he says, seated in the Senate antechamber, "but if we are to be an influence at all, we must." When the roll call buzzer burrs through the room, Vande Hoef, like the others, responds to his new job.

Across the spacious hallways of the capitol, Vande Hoef's Republican colleague, Representative Harold Van Maanen, a cattlefeeder by profession, sits in session, his wife-secretary, Luella, next to him. Somewhere in Iowa there's an invisible line that separates the northern from the southern United States. No Iowan ever kept slaves; but anybody who hails from south of the line carries more of a southern drawl than most Yankees. Van Maanen does. He's fifty-two years old, and he doesn't talk like a politician—what he lacks in slickness, he makes up for in sincerity.

For Van Maanen, it was the local public school board that ushered him into what is called "public life." He ran under the recommendation of his supposedly retiring father-in-law, who was then himself renominated for the school board, a turn of events that forced Tracy, Iowa, voters to choose between father and son-in-law. Son-in-law won by ten votes; father smiled.

He spent eighteen years on the local school board, from the time his daughter was a first-grader to the time his younger son graduated from high school. His experience on the board was significant, he says, and it helped him to decide to throw his hat into the district representative race when an ex-legislator, a personal friend, urged him to consider running. Like Vande Hoef, however, Van Maanen didn't make the decision easily.

At that time Harold Van Maanen felt somewhat inadequate; his own education had stopped at his high school graduation when the Korean conflict interfered. But he was always interested in the legislative process. Almost collared into running by a Republican committee from his home district in 1978, Van Maanen still

115

Senator Bass Van Gilst,
Representative Bill Dieleman,
Senator Richard Vande Hoef, and
Representative Harold Van Maanen:
serving two constituencies.

felt reluctant, until he was introduced to a successful legislator named Horace Daggett, a farmer by profession and a committed Christian. Daggett's urging made it even more difficult to look the other way.

"Through the prayers of my wife, Pastor Meuzelaar, and myself, we felt the Lord was opening the door for us." So the farm boy with no political background ran against a two-term incumbent, spent no more than $2,200, and rang doorbells around the district. He won.

"You've got to have credibility as a legislator before your faith means anything at all to others," he says today, in the middle of his second term. "People have to see Christ in your work." And that's not always an easy job. "There are times when you swallow hard and vote with your party. It's the nature of things here, because some compromise is always necessary, but it's not an easy thing to do."

Just west of Van Maanen's home district lies the town of Pella, and at the other end of the political spectrum sits Democratic Representative Bill Dieleman, presently in his fourth term. Dieleman married Emily Langstraat in 1951, just a year and one child prior to getting the call to the Korean conflict. In 1955, at twenty-four years of age, Bill Dieleman, Korean veteran, moved his family to Grand Rapids and started Calvin College, majoring in history. Although Dieleman, like his colleagues, was urged by others to run, his presence in the House is as much the result of his own prompting; he taught at Calvin Christian School in South Holland, Illinois, and at his own alma mater, Pella Christian High, for fifteen years, and he always recommended political involvement to his students. Today, he considers the plight of private schools an important issue, and he credits his own background in Christian schools for that commitment.

Twice elected to Pella's city council, he decided to run for the House seat of a friend, a Republican, who had decided against trying to return to the legislature.

117

"It's a real challenge," he says of the political life. "There's always something new, and there's the satisfaction of doing things that you know are right." Representative Dieleman looks like a politican. He has a youthful, handsome face and short, thick hair that stands up on his forehead. He speaks slowly, carefully, as if each of his words is being examined closely by some quality controller.

"Every area of life is important to a Christian. Government is something not simply to complain about, but, where and when you can, to change through political involvement. Too often we only contact our legislators when we have some complaint about government, he says. Dieleman says he was discouraged to see only one Christian Reformed person from his district attend an open hearing on parimutuel betting, a practice that he has personally opposed throughout his seven years at Des Moines. Several from his district spoke in favor of the legislation at the meeting, in spite of his notifying "concerned" groups within his area.

"Abortion stirs people up, but only at election time. I just wish that CRC members would take a more active role in politics—by letting me know how they feel about issues, for example. Too often, it doesn't happen."

The head of the CRC delegation, Senator Bass Van Gilst, agrees with his colleague, as do Van Maanen and Vande Hoef. Were it only Van Gilst who said it, we would have reason enough to listen to him. He's been in the Iowa Senate for seventeen years and has held positions such as Democratic Whip and Assistant Majority Leader. "I'm a Democrat because the first time I voted was in 1932, and as far as I was concerned there was only one choice—Franklin D. Roosevelt." He's seventy years old now, this son of an immigrant father, and he, too, is a farmer; he runs a diversified operation outside of Oskaloosa.

"Politics came natural to me," he says. "I'm a Calvinist through and through; I *had* to be active in politics because politics are important for Christians." It's not hard to see why Van Gilst was chosen as Whip; when he speaks, there is a determined force in his voice, a conviction that forces you almost to smile in admiration. "We're Calvinists," he says. "We have to run this government."

Unlike the others, Van Gilst lost his first political race. Encouraged to try again, however, he did. "It's always been my feeling that people vote for a voice. I vote my conviction. If they don't like my conviction, they'll vote me out next time around." Perhaps it was this philosophy that enabled him to forget the initial loss and to try again. And he won in the Democratic landslide of 1964. Ever since, Van Gilst has been a fixture in the Iowa Senate.

In 1964 he was in the consistory, and he says that he feels some people looked down on him for his interest in politics. "I think that kind of attitude is changing now, and I'm happy about it."

But if there's one weakness all these politicians sense in their church, it is political apathy, or antagonism—the feeling that politics is not a kingdom-calling. All admit, however, that attitudes are improving.

Despite their political differences, there's a remarkable similarity in the way each of them views their church. Each, for instance, insists that the great strength of the CRC is its insistence on biblical authority. And all of them explain that the difficult job facing us denominationally is balancing the strength of a powerful tradition over against the necessity of change and renewal. "We can't go back to the old sober faces," Van Maanen says, and Van Gilst agrees: "We need more emphasis on catechism, but more willingness to change on some things—close communion, the nature of the second service."

Vande Hoef says we have overemphasized one end

of a paradox for too long: "We can't be the salt of the earth if we insist we must 'come apart and be separate.' " And Dieleman, like the others, maintains that "finding new programs for youth involvement and community outreach" are necessary parts of the future work of the Christian Reformed Church.

Etched somewhere amid the classical antiquity of the Iowa capitol building are the words, "Where Law Ends Tyranny Begins." Four CRC politicians who spend a bit more than a hundred days per year in the regal splendor of the place know, however, that law itself is not the ultimate authority. But this confession does not make their jobs any less complicated, because they serve two constituencies: one, the assembly of voters in their respective districts; the other—sometimes at odds with the former—a sovereign Creator.

15

All Roads Lead to Gallup: Tony and Etta Aguayo

Sometime way back in the early days of this century, Francisco Aguayo took a last look at his homeland and, with his wife and family, headed north from Parral, Mexico, about 250 miles south of Juarez, to the new state of New Mexico in the United States of America. It was work he wanted, any kind of work to support his young and growing family. He found a coal mine in Gamerco, about five miles north of Gallup, and he settled his family there. In 1929, a boy, Anthony, the thirteenth of fifteen children, was born.

Three years after World War II, Frank Bylsma, a shipbuilder from Friesland, the Netherlands, put his wife, his four children, and his mother on a ship and took a last look at his homeland. They arrived in Quebec, unloaded their possessions, including the car they had brought along, and drove to Grand Rapids, Michigan, where relatives awaited their arrival in the new country. Frank Bylsma immigrated for his children, really, for opportunities he guessed they simply would not have in the old country. His oldest son, George, was already eighteen years old; Etta, only eight; Eldon, six; and the youngest, Mina, five. Grandma was eighty.

Early every Sunday morning, Tony Aguayo, along with the rest of the family, marched off to mass at the little Roman Catholic church on the dusty streets of Gamerco. He picked up the English language during the early years of his education in the village, and, when he was old enough for high school, his parents insisted he travel the five miles to Gallup, to the fine Roman Catholic high school, Sacred Heart. Religion, the church, the Roman Catholic faith, played a significant role in the Aguayo family life.

The Bylsmas established their home in southwest Grand Rapids and worshiped as a family at the Grandville Avenue Christian Reformed Church. Etta, like her brothers and sisters, learned the new language in school, out on the playground mostly, where her friends were her teachers. She attended Southwest Christian School and Grand Rapids Christian High, graduating in January 1959. Religion, the church, the Reformed faith—all played a significant part in the Bylsma family life, and, when Etta was ten or eleven, her ears turned every Saturday morning to the "Children's Bible Hour." She quietly, individually, accepted Christ as her Savior. No great fanfare hailed her decision; she didn't even tell her mother. But from that day on, she never questioned her relationship with her God.

In 1945, Tony Aguayo, just sixteen years old, tried to enlist in the army simply because he wanted to serve his country. But the army sent him back to finish high school. After graduation he enlisted for four years in the US Army Air Force and was sent to San Antonio, Texas, for basic training. The army put him in administrative school in Denver, Colorado, and then assigned him to the Pentagon in Washington, D.C. The place was full of administrative personnel, and the only opportunity he saw for advancement was in overseas duty. So he put in for transfer and was sent to the island of Guam, a place that seemed like paradise.

Etta Bylsma worked as a volunteer with the elderly at Pine Rest Christian Hospital one summer, like so many other CRC young women, and during her senior year at Christian High, she heard a career nurse speak about the opportunities and challenges of the nursing profession. Nursing sounded appealing to her, but three or four years of additional schooling seemed too much right then, so she enrolled in junior college in a Licensed Practical Nursing program. A year later she was changing dressings on patients, on staff at Blodgett Memorial Hospital in Grand Rapids.

Tony Aguayo didn't stay in Guam long. One warm night he was injured seriously in a motorcycle accident on the island. He spent two long weeks in a coma. For more than a year he was yo-yoed in and out of army hospitals—El Paso, Pearl Harbor—all the while receiving physical therapy for the slowly relenting grip of paralysis on his left side. In 1949 he was discharged, one year early, for medical reasons.

At twenty-one years old, Etta Bylsma realized that her frame of reference was no broader than Grand Rapids and a Christian Reformed world. It was time to leave, so she moved to Philadelphia, where she worked as a nurse at Delaware County Hospital. One night a patient asked her, almost out of the blue, if she were a Christian. When she said yes, the man said he could tell by the way she acted around him. It was exactly what she needed to hear. In experiencing a sense of her individual difference from others around her, she found something of what she was looking for in Philadelphia, her own identity. Grand Rapids had been too much a hall of mirrors before; now there was no particular reason to stay in Philadelphia. She returned to Blodgett.

Nearly two hundred war veterans—Indians, Mexi-

The Aguayo family:
a classic, textbook mixed marriage.

cans, Anglos—came home to Gallup in the late 40s, came home to no jobs, as if the country they had served, many of them in combat in Europe or the Pacific, had used them, then left them stranded on the high, dry plains of western New Mexico. Tony roamed the Southwest—coalminer, construction worker, bakery apprentice—trying to find some stable employment. Finally, more than a year of frustration later, the Korean conflict generated jobs at the Ft. Wingate Army Depot. The administrative certification he had earned in the service made him eligible for opening positions. He has been at Ft. Wingate for thirty years.

It was snowing hard in Michigan, and Frank Bylsma fretted some when he thought of his daughter's white Corvair convertible, packed solid with all of Etta's earthly belongings. He worried about her ever getting out of Grand Rapids, much less all the way down to Rehoboth, New Mexico, just ten miles east of Gallup; so he followed her out of town like a wilderness guide, and she made it—out of the city and all the way to the Southwest. Etta wanted to go to Rehoboth because her faith had matured and flourished, and she found herself willing to follow God's gentle tugging. When she arrived at Rehoboth, in January 1965, she felt herself part of a new loving family of nurses and aides.

Specialists in Albuquerque told Tony Aguayo that he had forty-eight hours to decide whether or not he wanted to keep his right leg. Tony and two others, returning from a ballgame in Farmington, New Mexico, had been struck, head-on, by a semitruck. Only Tony, his right leg crushed at the knee, had survived. The choice he had was not easy: either keep the leg and be faced with the possibility of nearly continuous hospitalization, or lose it. He called his mother, he called a priest, he asked the nurses—he wanted desperately for someone to tell him what to do, but no one would. Finally, he told the specialists to take his right leg off.

Ten years of suffering later, the pain in the stump had not relented. Captain Van Valkenberg, a medical officer with a missile battalion at Ft. Wingate Army Depot, advised Tony to see Dr. Vanden Bosch at Rehoboth Christian Hospital. When he checked in, Chaplain Cook told Tony, jokingly, that he was in a good place; he could take his pick of the nurses. A month passed in the little hospital. He chose Etta Bylsma, and Etta chose him.

Today, fifteen years later, the pain in the stump is pretty much a thing of the past, but Tony and Etta will tell you that life hasn't been a bowl of cherries. First, there was the initial Michigan homecoming. Picture it: Etta brings Tony Aguayo—a Mexican-American, a Catholic, a man ten years her elder—back home to her Frisian parents, her father, now somewhat hard of hearing and quite unable to communicate in English, a thoroughly Gereformeerde patriarch. "Here he is, Pa," she might have said as they stepped off the train in the Grand Rapids station. If you think that's a scene, how about the other end: Tony's mother, devout Roman Catholic, Spanish-speaking, hears the news of her son's desire to marry an Anglo girl, Christian Reformed, from Rehoboth. "She said, 'No!' " Tony says. "That's all, just no. Then she hit the roof."

But they were married (with parental approval) just a year after Tony left Rehoboth Hospital, but it was a year of discussion and counseling and learning on both sides. "We were a lot alike, really," Etta says. "When we had to explain our own faith, its doctrines, we found it more difficult than it should have been, probably, at least for two people brought up in the church."

Tony says he learned that the fundamentals, deep down, are not really that different. "The basic difference [between the Roman Catholic and Christian Reformed faiths] is the saints between God and man," he says, but he admits that he never put much faith in them anyway.

Tony Aguayo has been in the CRC for fifteen years now, and he finds the study of and belief in the Word of God to be a strength of his new church. But he has a list of weaknesses too. Basically, he says, "the old Dutch customs are too strict." Reared as he was in and around Gallup, a real sports town, Tony thinks, for instance, that the old prohibition against organized baseball on Sunday is more of a barrier between the CRC community and the Gallup people, more of a barrier than a mark of devotion or piety or any kind of testimony. "People just don't understand that," he says. "They say Rehoboth just thinks they're holier than everybody else."

Etta doesn't see these things in quite the same way, however, having been reared in her church. "I need a day of rest," she says. "I think Sunday should be a day apart from the rest of the week." When she speaks, she talks to Tony. This Sunday business isn't totally resolved yet.

Gallup is a long, string-bean city, the Indian capital of North America, maybe, although you might beg a fight from Flagstaff or any of a number of other places; at least it has more bargain turquoise jewelry outlets per capita than any other place on this continent. Gallup stretches out along historic US 66 like a lengthening shadow in a slow New Mexico sunset. The Aguayos have made Gallup their hometown, the home of their four children—Robert, Allen, Cynthia, and Marineta.

Tony and Etta Aguayo are a classic, textbook mixed marriage, a prototype of the kind both sets of immigrant parents would have certainly disapproved—some time longer than fifteen years ago, that is. But today, their smiles, their children's smiles, their home—all these things verify the oneness Tony and Etta have built on the firm foundation of faith.

16

Lillian Bode: Pioneer Missionary

When Lillian Bode folds her arms over her scrapbook, she holds more than eighty years of memories close to her. Inside, there are yellowed pictures of women in floppy hats, arms entwined, standing alongside steamships; there are black-and-white photos of Chinese Christians smiling their Sunday school best in front of a row of folding chairs; and there are colored landscapes of the mountains of Taiwan.

The scrapbook is the story of her lifelong devotion to missions and the story of her own personal preparation for the much greater life she sees coming closer each time the sun sets over the California sandhills just west of the trailer park where she and her sister live today, thousands of miles from the Orient. She knows she won't take the scrapbook along when she leaves, but she knows that some of those faces she'll surely see again.

And that's what makes her raise her fist when she tells you the story; that's what makes her point her thumb up in the air, time after time, as if she were some wartime flying ace signaling a series of victories.

Picture her in that pose as you listen to her tell her story.

My father was a preacher. My father and mother were married just a few years before the beginning of this century. They had a country church. The church was new, the parsonage was new, and the roads were not yet established. They had road horses, and they just drove across the prairie in Iowa.

I came into this world at the beginning of this century. Mother was a daughter of people in Illinois, and they had a lot of miscarriages, but somehow she lived— she was precious, you see? Then I came into the world —and I got sick with pneumonia. In those days if you had pneumonia, it was fatal. Mother said to herself, "How can I ever live without this child?"

And then she thought—"She could be a missionary!" At that moment she gave me to the Lord. I was just a baby, but I got better right away. She never told me this until years later when I came home on my first vacation from Bible school.

All through my life she held up mission work to me. She never told me to go into missions. When I was a teenager, we had Mission Fest—one whole day of preaching. Mother would see that I would go to the missionary's speech, and then, when I'd get home, I'd have to tell her all about it. She encouraged me in that way.

My mother and I both taught Sunday school classes when I grew older. We both had special mission envelopes in our Sunday school classes. Mother sent her special offerings to Miss Veenstra in Africa. I sent mine to China because in 1917 the China missionaries sent us information about the starvation in that country.

Later on, when I taught school in Sheboygan, Wisconsin, and in Holland, Iowa, I received a letter from Dr. Huizenga in China. Dr. Huizenga knew that our family was always very mission-minded. Whenever he toured the country, he would stay at our place overnight, and even use our car. His letter to me said, "We have ten children, maybe five grades. If you could come and teach them here in China, we wouldn't have to send them away from home. We hope you will do this."

I thought it would be wonderful. At the same time, I felt that I'd be watching people going into the temple to worship idols. I wouldn't have time to learn the language, and my heart would go out to those doomed Chinese people.

People said, "Well, you're single. You should go; it would be a nice experience. Go there for a year or two."

I decided that I would write Huizenga and tell him I was coming. Every Saturday I'd plan to do it, but when I'd try to write the letter, I'd just break down and cry—I just couldn't say yes.

I had never prepared for missions. I was a church member and a Sunday school teacher, but a missionary has to be more than that. So I asked myself, "Why didn't I ever prepare for missions?"

Six months went by. I was teeter-tottering all that time, and finally they sent me a steamship card for China. Well, at that time I *had* to decide—yes or no. I had already decided that if I didn't go to China, I would go to a Bible school. Our church had no Bible school then, and, of course, women were not allowed at the seminary.

Finally I decided I would write to Dr. Huizenga and tell him that it was off. I told Dad that I had decided to go to Bible school, and Dad said, "Yeah, you try it for a term." His fatherly strings were pulling. He didn't say no when I told him I wasn't going, but he wanted me to go. He was a member of our foreign mission board for over twenty years, and he loved mission work.

I went to Moody Bible Institute—three terms in a year. When I registered, I saw there was a missionary course, but I signed for a Bible course instead. That night I had no rest. I told myself—what if this opportunity [to go to China] should come again? So I went back the next day and told them I had registered in the wrong course of study—I had made a mistake. After that I had great peace of mind.

One of the courses we had was synthesis—Bible synthesis—maybe half a chapter of Matthew, but you had to read and reread that portion for seven hours in a week. That did wonders for me, reading the Bible that way, closely. My faith soared high. Before half the term was over, I had written the mission board, "Do you need a woman worker in China? I'm at Moody's and if all goes well, the next year I'll be graduating. I am glad to offer my services."

Dr. Henry Beets was then secretary of missions. He wrote me, "We have your name down, and when you're ready to go, you can go."

It was 1926 when I went. I thought to myself, the Catholic priests never have furloughs. I am single too. God has done so much for me, I'd like to spend the rest of my life in China. And I went. Seven of us went, three couples, and I was the single one.

We went to the university in Nanking to do language study. Altogether, there were about sixty or seventy of us from different churches for one year of language study. But when the year came to an end, there was a war on—a big army marching up from the south. People said not to worry because the armies didn't pay any attention to foreigners. But they said we must be prepared anyway. They told us to put all our things in our trunks and lock the trunks in the closets, just in case the soldiers would come in.

One Sunday night we could hear machine guns. We didn't even undress for bed because the consul told us not to. At dawn we had orders to go to the Yangtze River to meet a gunboat coming for us.

Betsy Ploeg was there. She was on the Methodist board, but she was from Grand Rapids. I knew her. The two of us were taken on this motorcycle with a cab attached. Betsy sat on the bottom with me on her lap, and then the two suitcases and a steamer blanket.

Lillian Bode:
first lady of the China mission.

We had to stop when the army was passing by—one, two, three, four. We looked up, and there was this big sign with heads hanging of those who had been found guilty of rebellion. We wondered whether we would even get to our boat, but we made it.

All the Americans were on the boat. The next day was to have been the day for our exams, so we had books along to study. Our missionaries were there too—Mrs. Huizenga and the children. Toward evening a flagman sent a message that the army had turned against foreigners; some missionaries had been killed. They told us we should make tracks for Shanghai, where we could get picked up by a river steamer.

I didn't want to go. I felt that I'd just like to run into the country and stay with a Chinese family. I could learn the language and the customs by staying with them.

But here I was, already going home. We went to Shanghai, and on the way we were shot at. We had to get under the tables and on the floor.

Things weren't much better in Shanghai. The American consulate had called everyone in because they were afraid it would be like the Boxer Rebellion. We had mission meetings every day to try to decide what to do. We decided that people close to furlough should leave, but those who had just come should stay. This was fine with me.

Finally, we got a cable from home that said if it was dangerous, we shouldn't be afraid of coming home. The mission board said they had a place for every missionary to work.

I was very disappointed because I wanted to stay in China. But someone said to me, "To obey is better than sacrifice." So I went home trying to get comfort. I was home for two years. I was disappointed when others could stay, but the CRC missionaries went home.

I was able to go back again, however, for several

years before the war; but when the war came, we all returned home again, and I did city mission work in Grand Rapids. Rev. De Korne called me later.

I wanted to go to some heathen place somewhere, where I could really work. De Korne said that Zuni needed a teacher—I might think about that. I taught in Zuni for three and a half years, and I thought that was just it. I liked it there.

But every year two board members would come to visit. They would say, "Well, you're enjoying yourself here—you had better forget about China." And I did ask the Lord to take it out of my heart. If this was his will, then I should be subject to it.

But the desire wasn't taken away; it was like a stone on my heart! Every board meeting I'd talk to the visitors, and, when they were gone, they'd get a letter from me with the same idea. Finally they asked me to come to visit with them in Grand Rapids.

Years ago I knew most of the board members, and I listened to them talk about my idea for a while, and finally I said, "Well, if I could have a word? We were in China years ago; we worked with the Chinese. The Chinese are still there on the mainland, but there are also plenty of Chinese on Taiwan and in the Philippines. Taiwan appeals to me. They are still our field. Why don't we call them the 'dispersed Chinese'? That would give the field a different appearance. It would be better."

"Now you'll have to go out, and we'll vote on it," they said. They had a big circle of dominies, and I guess others too. But I was outside the door and I wanted to hear. They said, "All in favor?" and there was a big "Aye!" "Opposed?" and there was no sound. So I was the first one to go to Taiwan, alone.

I quickly found a woman who knew the Bible well to assist me, and we could start. Some Taiwanese preachers came to us and said they had heard we were looking for places to start. "There's a place about an hour and a half from Taipei—five families, country people. They would like to have a church. We will pay for the rent of a building if you can get your mission board to pay for the preacher.'' That was the bargain.

We started with a morning service at noon. The farmers were barefooted Taiwanese with pointed hats; they would bring a little bag with meat and rice and vegetable, and they'd have dinner with their friends on the street. Then they'd come back for song service and a second service. By the end of the first year the place was too small, so they moved to a larger building. Today, it's a fine Taiwanese church.

We would go there by bus and often meet soldiers from the air base. So one day we got off the bus at the base and passed out tracts. We met a woman there— she could speak very good English—and she was the chief pilot's wife. She told us she had been to the Catholic church, but she didn't think it was the right way. ''Won't you come and teach some of us?'' she asked.

For two years we met there with the women of the base, and today there's a church there too, a Sunday school, and youth meetings. We are praying for a preacher who will meet the needs of the church on the base. They need a preacher.

I knew a woman, a single Lutheran woman about my age, who had six hours given to her in a private college—six hours to teach English. The head of that college was a Christian; he thought that students should hear the gospel. The course was called ''Ancient Classics'' because if the students thought it was Christianity, they wouldn't want it. She gave me six hours to teach too. Sooner or later we moved that student group into a tent and started working there with families too, for several years. Finally we moved into a new church on Nanking Road. Today that's a thriving church.

I was in Taiwan for six years alone; by the time the men finally came, I had six preaching places. When we couldn't get the men from other denominations, I'd preach myself.

We heard that high up in the mountains there were mainlanders, Chinese refugees, working in a big gold mine. They had a library, a high school, a grade school, and even tennis courts—everything but a church. Those people in the mountains were highly educated, university graduates—men as well as women, and all mainlanders. So we took a lunch along, and we ate it in a shady place and went door-to-door to see if there were any Christians, or if there were any who would like to hear the gospel.

We kept going back there. One day the head of the mine came to talk to us. He told us that he knew we were concerned about his people. He said, "We have a library room; you can go there and eat your lunch, or we have a place where you can eat. And if you want any meetings, you can use that room too. There are benches there; it's a large room."

We started meetings there, and, finally, Sundays we'd send up a preaching elder. But these people were highly educated Chinese—who was I to talk to them? We'd lean hard on the Lord every time my Bible woman and I would go there.

The mine was the largest gold mine in the Orient, and they told us that every stone had gold in it. But we prayed that the Lord would become more precious to them than gold.

And we found Christians! One woman opened the door—"Oh," she said, "I'm so glad to see you. I haven't been in church for six years." Well, it turned out that this woman had taken voice lessons. "Could you start a choir?" I asked her. "The singing isn't good on Sunday. You can start." She did. And she found a man from Peking, mainland China. He had once directed the *Messiah* there.

She got him interested, and he had friends from the mainland who had trained voices, and when Christmas came, we had seventeen numbers from the *Messiah*—solos included!

For the Christmas program, they also acted out the parable of the prodigal son, and the Sunday school children memorized Scripture—Luke 2—and they gave presents. It was such a program! And suddenly, there came old Saint Nick! Oh, we hung our heads! You now, you don't teach those things, but they hear about them, and they think that's the thing to do. They just thought that Santa Claus was part of *our* Christmas!

One of the Christians—they were so devoted, wonderful Christians—just got up and said, "I want you children to know that this Santa Claus is not Christmas. It's just a happy story. He brings presents, but Christmas is the birth of Jesus, who died for us on the cross. He's your Savior—our Savior." She made it so clear that there was no mistake. You couldn't feel bad anymore.

They have their own church now.

The last church was 12th Street in Taipei. I went there three times after I retired—for a few months each time, and the last time I stayed on two years.

Sixty-five years—that's the limit, you know. Then you go home, you retire. But I was well. I knew the language. I knew the customs. I knew all our mission stations because I had started them all. I thought, "If I go home, I think it is a sin! I've got this all now. There's no reason I can't stay on."

I asked the board and the missionaries, and nobody said no, so I stayed on eight years more—without furlough. And then more missionaries came on.

But it got so the places were all four floors high, and I couldn't do it anymore. The people would close the door and you couldn't get in. You would say, "I'm from the church," and they'd say, "Oh, ah—goodby!" When you're young, you can do it—you can think of ways and you can go up stairs, but I couldn't do it anymore.

And now there's mainland China. They wrote about it in *The Banner* —did you see that? And there was an article in *The Banner* that said how badly we need more people to go into missions, how there are positions that are not being filled. The need is there, but not enough are going to spread the gospel.

Sometimes I think I still have some good years yet, you know—maybe I could go again. But maybe not, maybe not. . . .

But you write that, will you? You write how there's need for more people in missions, *and* there are people who need the gospel.

You write about how much we need more men and women in missions today.

You write that.

17

Dick and Joan Ostling

The Kuyperians among us like to insist that all of life is religion, that belief isn't simply one segment of the whole or some separate Sabbath Day's doing. But Kuyperian thought can hardly be said to dominate the skyline of Western thought; not everyone believes that life is religion, of course, despite our holding forth. Apparently the editors of *Time* magazine don't take the notion seriously—if indeed they have ever heard our Kuyperians say it: religion, in their magazine, merits consideration similar to and next to the fields of science, education, behavior, and the sexes—just another section, a separate section, in the "back of the book," as *Time* staffers call that part of the magazine.

Richard Ostling edits the Religion section of *Time* magazine. He is the only fulltime religion writer for a national magazine in North America. He is familiar with the Kuyperian argument; it's his business to be familiar with theology and theological argument. It's his business to read Barth and Bonhoeffer, to know about Catholic Pentecostalism and the roots of the Islamic revival. Religion is his business. Religion, in a sense, is his life.

The name *Ostling* is not Dutch, but Swedish. Dick Ostling and his wife, Joan, do not trace their blood lineage back to Scholte or Van Raalte. They have been members of the Ridgewood (New Jersey) Christian Reformed Church for nearly twelve years, but the path they took to get there winds through a maze of parental affiliations and personal decisions, not unlike their own tree-lined street meanders through the fine old suburb of Ridgewood.

Joan's maternal grandfather, an Englishman, was reared as an Anglican but converted to the Baptist faith in America. He served the Christian and Missionary Alliance as a missionary to India and the American Baptist Convention in a parish ministry in rural Pennsylvania. Most of Joan's theological heritage, however, is Pennsylvania Dutch—which is not Dutch, but German. She grew up in an Evangelical Congregational church. Her mother, still a Baptist at heart, insisted that her three children be baptized by immersion, despite the fact that the congregation, and the pastor for that matter, had never witnessed such an event.

The church rented the baptistry of a local Baptist congregation. "Usually you wear a white robe in the water, but my mother had me wear a jersey with broad red, white, and blue stripes," Joan remembers. The Evangelical Congregational preacher had never dunked a soul before. He pushed Joan down, following her mother's instructions. "I came up looking like the flag," she remembers.

Four years later, Joan decided to attend Wheaton College. She joined a local Episcopal church, where the movement and beauty of the liturgy triggered what she calls "a very quiet and very powerful presence within me."

"There's a certain way in which God is objectified in liturgy," she says. "The repetition of prayers, the phrasing—it had a way of capturing me. I can't tell you why." When she and Dick were married in 1967, she was Episcopalian.

Dick Ostling's father is a lifelong member of a Congregational church in Connecticut, despite the fact that he attended a Baptist church in New York for over thirty years. Dick says his father felt no need to be rebaptized; therefore, he never joined the Baptist church.

Dick Ostling was reared in this American Baptist church in Endicott, New York, a middle-of-the-road congregation in perhaps the most liberal denomination in the Baptist family of churches. He was baptized at twelve, but not because of some sudden flash; it was, as he puts it, more of an "acculturation of religion."

While at the University of Michigan, Ostling attended the CRC Campus Chapel, as did many of his friends who associated, as he did, with the Inter-Varsity program. But in 1967 Dick Ostling was, at least by culture, a Baptist.

"You might say we were classic church shoppers," he says, remembering the months following their marriage. He was news editor at *Christianity Today*; Joan was a writer for the US Information Agency. In 1969 *Time* hired him as a correspondent specializing in religion, and the Ostlings moved from Washington, D.C., to the New York City area.

"We compromised," Joan says, speaking of churches. "Ridgewood CRC stood somewhere between the Episcopal and Baptist churches." She laughs when she admits it, conscious that her characterization makes the decision sound as deliberated as the choice of a restaurant for Saturday night dinner.

Simply, Ridgewood CRC fulfilled their desires for a church: theologically orthodox, an acceptable level of music, a certain liturgical style for Joan, sound preaching for Dick. "We were looking for a combining of doctrinal orthodoxy with some social compassion," Dick says, "both within the pulpit and within the lay work. We were pleased to find that social responsibility is a significant part of the CRC."

If the Ostlings' vision of a church home seems as objective as some job description, Joan and Dick Ostling are quick to point out that they lack what they call "the CRC tribal instinct," the ethnic and cultural inclusiveness that characterizes many of us who have been born and reared within the Dutch Reformed tradition.

"We are evangelical Protestants who happen to have found a home in the CRC," Dick says. "And that's fairly unusual, even ironic, because evangelicalism, which is often called fundamentalism, is almost a swear word in the CRC. But CRCs are evangelicals without knowing or recognizing it."

Listening to Dick Ostling talk is like reading a fine essay. His occupation is building and communicating sound ideas, and his tools are words. He is a skilled craftsman. "Evangelicalism," he explains, "is a reactionary movement. It has reacted against the rise of liberal theologies in the denominational institutions of a generation ago. Reactionary psychology produces all kinds of strange things, intellectually and spiritually. But the CRC has never yet had to deal with liberalism, at least the kind of liberalism that other orthodox Protestant churches have had to deal with in the past, so the Christian Reformed Church has had the luxury of sitting back and disdaining the evangelicals."

The Ostlings' view of the Christian Reformed Church is unique and instructive. To many of us—too many—the Ostlings are still "outsiders," not members of the tribe. And it is that tribal spirit which bothers and often perplexes them. "If the CRC is to become an American not a Dutch denomination, it must fight the battles of evangelicalism—inerrancy, for instance. If it wants to be part of the North American Protestant landscape someday, it has to engage in those battles. In other words, is the CRC going to fall into some mindless version of inerrancy, or can it articulate a conservative commitment to Scripture, to biblical authority, which prevents the inroads of a basically liberal theology, but yet is not the same as the views of inerrancy it does not like? This is a very important

142

Dick and Joan Ostling:
"classic church shoppers."

question for the CRC to face." He does not pound the coffee table when he speaks; his hands barely move. Authority rides the exposition of the argument.

Both Joan and Dick see the isolation of the tribe as an inherent danger of the Christian school system; their two daughters are currently in public school. "Our choice of school varies according to our academic assessment of the local public and Christian schools, and the needs, academic and spiritual, of each child," says Joan. "We have used the Christian schools already and may again, but I don't feel a wholly parochial education is always healthy. A child must learn, as part of his education, to live as a Christian in the world at large. It is difficult to do this with the isolation inherent in a parochial school system."

It may be a result of the studied objectivity of journalism, but when the Ostlings speak of the CRC, they use the words *it* and *they,* even when they list the strengths of the church. "We appreciate the strong position they [the CRC] take against abortion, despite the tremendous pressure to be in favor of it in Protestantism. Although millions oppose abortion, relatively few denominations have taken a strong stand against it," Dick says.

The Ostlings also appreciate the sponsoring of many special service agencies—Bethany Christian Services, for example. They feel such agencies illustrate a high quality of institutional life. Also, they appreciate the distinctive intellectual tradition of the CRC. "Even when we don't agree," Joan says, "we respect it."

The Ostlings live in a sturdy house on a hill in Ridgewood, New Jersey. Joan homemakes today, while trying to decide whether to complete her doctoral dissertation in English at NYU. Their two daughters, Margaret and Elizabeth, both play the harpsichord that stands on the hardwood floor of the living room.

Across the street from the house, the commuter train Dick takes to work in the city runs past, then coasts down the suburban hills and bullies its way into New York. On a clear day you can probably sketch the skyline of the city from the Ostlings' front porch.

It is not Grand Rapids; surely, it is not Zeeland. It is not even old Paterson. And Dick and Joan Ostling cannot swap tribal pedigrees with you, because way-back-when their uncles didn't go to Calvin with yours.

Dick says that sometimes the tribal thing is to him a puzzle, even though it is his business to know the many varieties of Christianity. In a sense tribalism puts the CRC in a perplexing position. "It won't affiliate with the World Council of Churches, on the left, or the National Association of Evangelicals, on the right. The CRC stands apart from right-wing and left-wing Protestantism, yet it affiliates closely with some of the most theologically bizarre institutions on the globe." He shakes his head, laughs. "Presbyterians, Episcopalians, Methodists—I know what these people are up to, and I can guess where things are heading. But sometimes the CRC is a puzzle to me, even though I've been in it for almost twelve years."

Millions of Americans read Dick Ostling. Religion is his business, and understanding the nuances of the evangelical world is his specialty. His background is the culture of that world; both he and Joan are on loan to us, perhaps.

"If the CRC doesn't 'go American,' it's going to die. Every ethnic denomination has faced this—the CRC is just the latest, perhaps. And yet, you lose the good points when you Americanize. The intellectual and spiritual qualities of the CRC have been preserved by its isolation from the rest of Christendom.

"The problem that I fear is it may be apart ethnically more than spiritually. Ethnicity is not as important as the theology or spirituality of the church. It may give up the latter for the former. But then it will become a ghetto without a Christian rationale for its apartness."

We'll not get the Ostlings to use *we* instead of *they* by

carving them some wooden shoes. It's not that easy. If most of us want the rest of us to be like most of us, all of us will have to "reculturize" a bit, and that may be painful, to all of us. No one ever said it would be easy.

Dick and Joan Ostling know that the CRC is today, for better or worse, a North American denomination rooted in a Dutch variation of the theology of John Calvin, a Frenchman who, incidentally, lived in Switzerland.

18

The Marly Visser Farm, Orange City, Iowa

Marly Visser can chuckle about Sietze Buning, even though his father's dairy, where he grew up, is no more than a few pastures from the Buning homestead, and even though their families are old friends from the Middleburg church. And he can laugh at the short-sightedness of "Calvinist farming," even though he meets regularly with a Christian Farmers Organization, even though he knows that the issues they talk about—minimum tillage, herbicides, confinements— may be equally comical in retrospect. And he can laugh, even though he is as clearly committed to the integration of his confession and his profession as was Sietze's own generation.

Marly Visser operates what he describes as a "little bigger than average" hog setup on the long-drawn plains of Northwest Iowa. Today it may be a typical Iowa farm; there is no old hulking barn here anymore, just a series of frame buildings, some modern in design and function, specially designated to handle the job of farrowing and finishing hogs.

Farthest to the east is what Visser calls the "ges-tating building"; what it really is is the palace of the six boars he employs to impregnate his ninety sows. Right next door to the west is the farrowing shed, the mater-nity ward where Marly plays midwife to the sows,

Marly Visser:
vet, mechanic, agronomist,
gambler, accountant.

each twice yearly, where most every one of the ninety brings a dozen or so piglets into the world, and where he cuts back the little teeth and tails, then vaccinates the little things against a variety of barnyard maladies, and finally weans them from Mother.

A month later, when the little critters fatten to twenty pounds, he hauls them all the way over to a converted chicken coop he calls the "nursery"—a heated, insulated building separated into about a dozen sections, equipped with individual water spigots for efficiency and cleanliness, and underlaid with a waste system that keeps the place about as neat as anyone could imagine a hog pen to be. Actually, the pigs are housetrained in the nursery, that's right, *housetrained*—you might have thought the idea of a clean pig was an oxymoron, a kind of contradiction in terms.

About two months or thirty pounds later, they are herded off to the "finishing house." When you step into this place—Marly's favorite building—you look across a range of white Yorkshire backs, almost as if you were looking over a room full of baldheaded men. Here, both feed and water are dispensed at the leisure of the hogs, and manure—again, conscientiously placed by the hogs—is quickly escorted away mechanically. There are no pitchforks in the finishing house.

You might, in fact, call the place a casino; "finishing house" certainly sounds better, but the whole layout is a kind of casino, really. A modern hog farmer, in addition to having to be a vet, a mechanic, and an agronomist, must be something of a gambler. When the hogs grow up and out to 220 pounds of ham, they *must* be marketed—there's no choice involved, just a matter of days.

And the market, in case you didn't know, has daily price changes. Unlike your local A & P, the market prices occasionally, and not always predictably, take extended nosedives that can threaten an entire operation; for a farmer like Marly Visser, who has always wanted the family farm, the market threatens an entire way of life. Not only when the hogs go off, but how they are sold becomes something of an educated guessing game, something of a continuous gamble. Simply, Marly's gains have to offset his losses. You can add "accountant" to that list of vocations prerequisite to modern farming.

Marly and Esther Visser live in a large, comfortable farmhouse, but there's no pretention in it—it's a home. Maybe it's hard to be pretentious with a couple hundred hogs no more than fifty yards away, but even a quick trip around Northwest Iowa will tell you that it can be done. In the Vissers' case, modesty and cleanliness are a measured response to the concept of farmer as steward and as caretaker, not owner, of God's fertile land.

And it's what they have always wanted. Ever since Marly spotted Esther, then a timid little ninth grader on the bus to Western Christian High in Hull, ever since Marly was old enough to love the way of life his father showed him, through a liberal arts college education and two army years in Germany, it was always this, always the farm. "You can take the boy off the farm," he says, "but you don't always take the farm out of the boy."

"We think we're such big shots sometimes, especially we Reformed people—we have a lot of answers. Then something like this comes along and it brings us down to nothing, humbles us in the face of a sovereign God." The *something* Marly speaks of happened just three months ago at harvesttime, the first day of October. But to the Vissers, life before that day seems now to have been a whole different age, a time without questions, in a life as predictable as the inevitable march of the seasons across the windswept plains. Their own two-year-old boy, Ricky, as beautiful as any two-year-old, was killed, suddenly, tragically, horribly, in an accident that could have occurred only on a farm, only in the very middle of that way of life that Marly had dreamed of since he himself was a boy.

"No matter what you say," he says, "you're never ready for it. And when it comes, it shakes you; it shakes the best of you." The framed 8 x 10 in the living room is as real to them as the vivid, unforgettable image of a lifeless body, but today they speak openly about it, courageously, with a commitment that is real and reassuring because it has stood the greatest human test, the test of Job, and it has held firm.

"That night I remember asking myself about what kind of God I worshiped—about whether he was really in control—the sovereignty of God." He says it was the catechism that threatened him, the same catechism he had grown to respect and love, even as a teenager. It was the sovereignty of God and an unending litany of whys. Ricky's death hit him directly at the source of his strength; it made his greatest comfort a prison of doubt and anxiety.

It's the agonizing paradox painfully familiar to everyone who worships a sovereign Lord. To Jacob Arminius it was not a paradox but a dilemma that necessitated a choice, a choice against sovereignty; to Herman Melville it became a ghastly lifelong obsession: Does a sovereign God create evil? How can a loving God allow such terrible death? If God controls our lives, then didn't he cause this thing to happen? The question itself has been phrased in as many ways as there are languages—and in the hospital room, at the cemetery, in the middle of tears, there are no easy answers, no Band-Aid quips to stop the flow of anguish.

"People would say we aren't supposed to question things," he says, shaking his head. "Baloney! Hundreds of times David would go back to the Lord and say 'Why? Why? Why?' It's just not so easy to be submissive then."

*Life goes on
at the Visser farm.*

Today, three months later, he can speak of *then* with a settled and wider perspective, even if, as he admits, the questions still remain. And what was it that gave him and Esther the awesome strength needed simply to go on living? "The Word," he says. "We had been reading from Isaiah, and we had to go back to the Word." It was the comfort of Isaiah 40:

> See, the Sovereign Lord comes with power
>   and his arm rules for him.
> See, his reward is with him,
>   and his recompense accompanies him.
> He tends his flock like a shepherd:
>   He gathers the lambs in his arms
> and carries them close to his heart;
>   he gently leads those that have young.

Today, he speaks clearly. "You've got to take it 100 percent," he says. "If I want my God to be sovereign over the cemetery when he comes again, if I want him to raise that little body, then I also have to be able to say that he was in control on the first day of October." His eyes are piercing.

The Visser family, suddenly broken, was sustained by the wider family of God. "It's a tremendous thing," he says, "to have people standing behind you, telling you that it's all true—telling you that they know you've got a thousand questions. That was great. Just to be there, you know? They didn't even have to say anything, just that we knew they were there." Daily the mail carrier brought sympathy and strength from across the country—Florida, California, Montana.

And the whole thing changed Marly Visser. It's taken his love for the catechism and transformed it somehow. "You might say I'm more of a pietist—more aware of God, more aware of personal, daily fellowship. I loved the catechism before, kind of rationally, you know? But now I *know* God is sovereign."

For a few weeks after the accident, he says, he was full of nearly irrepressible urges to preach, even angrily. It was the harvest season, and "if everything's going well—the machinery's working the way it should—a farmer's got some time to think while he's working." While combining corn, he'd see a car pass his home. "I wanted to yell out at the driver, pull him from the car, shake my fist, and say, 'Hey, man, are you living covenantally with your God?' " Ricky's death has had that kind of effect.

And what of tomorrow? "People ask us," he says, "how we're doing." Sometimes, in some places, such a question is meant to make conversation, but not at the Vissers. "I tell them that theologically, spiritually, we're at rest. Salvation is assured. But I sure do miss the little guy." And when he says it, you smile, even laugh, at the way he says it because a smile covers the immense hole which, although deep and black, is not bottomless.

Ten days after Ricky's death the Vissers were blessed with a new baby girl, both mother and child healthy and strong. "Our other three kids were all a week early; Shari was a week late," Esther says, across the table from Marly, the baby in her arms.

You can't tell an Iowa farmer that for him winter is just one long vacation, but you surely can use up the better part of a January afternoon drinking coffee and talking at the Vissers. If you're smart, you won't hang around too long, or you're likely to get a shovel or a pitchfork volunteered to you. Because life goes on at the Vissers, and that fact itself is a gift of grace. If you don't know it already, Marly and Esther will tell you that it is, certainly.

19

Boet Gilde and the Obdurate

Man was originally formed after the image of God. His understanding was adorned with a true and saving knowledge of his Creator, and of spiritual things; his heart and will were upright, all his affections pure, and the whole man was holy. But, revolting from God by the instigation of the devil and by his own free will, he forfeited these excellent gifts; and in the place thereof became involved in blindness of mind, horrible darkness, vanity, and perverseness of judgment; became wicked, rebellious, and obdurate in heart and will, and impure in his affections.

(The Canons of Dort, III/IV, Article 1)

In West Palm Beach, Florida, the July night descends in darkness and covers the streets like a thick, wet blanket of heat. By midnight or one, the cleaning people have left the downtown shops, the middle-class theatergoers have driven their Chevys home to their bedroom communities, the last of the late-night officeworkers quit and retire, and the streets of the city are forfeited to men and women whose only joy is bellying up to seedy bars, to prostitutes and nightclub owners, to the chronically unemployed, the street punks, and the criminals.

Streets by day flowing with traffice evolve into empty tunnels that run through the darkened offices and locked-up department stores. Traffic lights shift gears for the night, flashing reds and yellows to the few cars that cross their jurisdiction. What traffic there is appears different: there are more taxis per capita, more heavy cars with rearends jacked up into the air, more pickups, more wrecks, more hotrods with loud mufflers and wide rear tires.

By three, West Palm Beach, like all our cities and many smaller towns, becomes a netherworld. The streets turn ugly, and anyone walking or driving seems an aberration and therefore suspect. At three in the morning, two groups vie for control of the streets: one of them, the police, represents us, takes home pay from our taxes; the other, purely nocturnal, more bold than wary, less smart than sinister, fills up our courtrooms, emblazons our newspapers with lurid, violent headlines, threatens us in the safety of our homes.

Ayatollahs equate Western culture with criminals and perverts; communists vilify us for our excesses; European media ridicule us for our inability to control ourselves. But we don't need outsiders to deliver jeremiads. We know that in too many places on this continent, fear itself holds a knife to our throats; crime imprisons us behind dead-bolt locks.

Boet Gilde, a fifteen-year veteran of the West Palm Beach police force, supervisor of the twelve squad cars that run the streets of the city after midnight, knows the antithesis better than most of us. Evil is no more clearly personified than in rapists, hookers, dope peddlers, burglars carrying death itself in their belts. To Boet Gilde, the enemy is an unidentified suspect in a stolen car, an intruder who has broken a window to gain entrance to a warehouse and still waits inside. When Boet Gilde straps on the belt laden with intimidators—a nightstick/flashlight, Mace, a police revolver—he does so with the knowledge that his job is a veritable battle in which he could be the loser. He has already lost colleagues to the war.

West Palm Beach, incorporated in 1894, was once a city on "the other side of the tracks"—the servants' quarters for the wealthy, the extremely wealthy, who built plush residences on the narrow strip of sand known as Palm Beach. Only the rich, the very rich, could live in Palm Beach. Their cooks, butlers, grooms, the cleaning women and the nannies whose services made possible the leisure extravagance of the idle rich—all of the "help" lived across the intercoastal waterway in West Palm. Years later something of the radical demarcation still exists, and pockets of West Palm Beach today carry the stigma of "ghetto."

But the problems of West Palm have been compounded by more recent events. Cuba's "floating flotilla" dumped thousands of immigrants—some of them less than desirable citizens—into the laps of all the coastal Florida cities. Haitians, running from economic starvation in their own country, add to the unemployed and complicate an already complex ethnic tension. And every winter thousands flock to Florida to escape northern winters. We have a tendency to think of "snowbirds" as retired and wealthy; but many others somehow manage to move south as well—bums, transients, criminals. Finally, drug traffic, higher in southern Florida than anywhere in the States, multiplies criminal activity, and the internecine warfare of the traffickers leaves bloody tracks throughout the community.

Boet Gilde faces that kind of world when he supervises night duty in West Palm. We pay people like Boet Gilde to do a job that few of us have the courage, the strength, the will to do ourselves; that is, we have hired him to ride shotgun for us through an area that has the fourth highest rate of crime per capita of any municipality in the United States.

"You can't be lax or you may be killed," he says, behind the wheel of the Dodge squad, the one with the word *Supervisor* printed in black letters above the front tires. Boet Gilde, nearly fifty, is a slight man, thin, well-groomed, his light brown hair combed neatly, short, police-short. His speech is a hybrid of accents: there is the thick *the* of his native Dutch language, and there are drawn-out vowel sounds of a southern dialect —"haowse" for house.

When he speaks to his patrolmen during the briefing —the "lineup"—he seems almost quiet, unpretentious. He looks over a cast of men much younger than he is, many of them in their early twenties, and he runs through the list of stolen vehicles and known criminals they should be watching for during their shift: "Richard Donald Foreman, white male, dangerous, thought to be on foot," he explains, and they note the description in their books. The men crack jokes in offensive language; they seem light-spirited, jocular, as they sit in classroom chairs in the precinct building, listening to Gilde's evening recital.

When they leave, he thumbs through complaint cards and arrest reports, looking for occurrences which may affect his own shift. An hour later, perhaps, he is on the road himself. His job is essentially supervision, watching the men under him to be sure that they do their job well. In addition, he is a kind of "rover," free to help out at will when the action calls for backup. He carries a black piece of luggage in the back seat, a kit for light detective work—powder for fingerprints, a camera for documentation.

There is a strange kind of community among the night owls. Boet Gilde knows prostitutes personally; he works at maintaining relationships with topless-bar owners. He calls them his friends because he needs their trust to do his job. He needs informers, street-wise characters who are willing to swap information when circumstances necessitate. It takes years of work to establish himself in their trust, and he prides himself in it. When he stops at a Dunkin' Donuts for coffee, the owner himself steps out of the back and

Boet Gilde:
giving a bum a Burger King hamburg.

puts his elbows up on the counter next to him. They swap stories, and laugh.

Officer Gilde knows the city at night. He knows the faces on the street, the men who mill around outside of bars, the cars that crawl like prowlers over semi-deserted streets. He knows the way office buildings look at night. He knows who parks on what street and when. And when something strikes him as strange—a different car, a light not normally left on, a door ajar—he investigates. His experience on the force has taught him to be cautious but strong.

He respects strength and despises weakness. He learned it already in adolescence, three and one-half years in a Japanese work camp in Indonesia. He saw men killed, shot dead for attempting to escape. One day the Japanese lined up the entire camp, hundreds of women and children. The commanding officer had discovered that one of his men had cohabited with a woman prisoner. The guilty man stood, hands bound, before the entire compound, the prisoners in rows in front, the Japanese in rows behind. And the commanding officer proceeded to kill his own man with his bare hands, beating and kicking him until the man's life was gone, until the man's screaming concluded. Boet Gilde learned that in order to live, strength—internal strength, the power of the will—is more than simply useful, it is a requirement.

He came to America with nothing but a sponsor and maybe forty dollars in his pocket. He took odd jobs, anything to create a new life in a new country—janitor, trash collector, license inspector—until he found himself in a position to become a policeman. He has no pity for those who refuse to sweat like he did, and even in his present job he relies on himself more than on others.

"I was very idealistic when I came into this job," he says. "I thought that being a policeman was something like being an elder, a big responsibility available only

160

to those who live with commitment to their job.'' But he says he has become disillusioned. ''Policemen are no better than anyone else. They are like the society that produces them—no better, no worse.''

The Japanese work camp, the long pull to economic independence, the fifteen years of street patrols—all of these have made Boet Gilde into a man of deep and clear commitments. His world is a world of clear contrasts—few shades of gray. He despises the legal system in this country. ''Policemen don't believe in rehabilitation. We see the criminals too often, time and time again, right back on the streets.'' Judges, lawyers, the court itself has frustrated his work too often, and he feels very strongly that the legal system does more to perpetuate crime than free us from being held hostage by the criminal. ''Plea bargaining, the time that it takes to get a case to court—too often everything works against my job. Two years after an arrest the case finally may come before the court. Then the lawyer expects you to remember every detail of one of a hundred cases you see in that time.''

Boet Gilde feels the way he does because he has been through it too often. ''It burns policemen out,'' he says. ''They start asking themselves what they are doing it for, and that's when the men stop caring.'' His Dodge wanders down back streets, past the back doors of shopping centers, as he makes his claims. He speaks forcefully, as conscious of the controversial nature of his appraisal as he is convinced of the truth of his convictions. ''It galls me no end,'' he says.

Commitment is important for Boet Gilde. Recently, when his church suffered through some internal problems and several members departed for other congregations or denominations, the Gildes stayed on. ''Too many people go for the preacher,'' he says.

But his own commitment does not inhibit him from speaking his mind. He feels that the church sometimes lends itself too much for the sake of entertainment these days, bending over backwards to accommodate or be relevant to youth. But he is committed to his church, even when he feels somehow at odds with the manner in which the church's program is being carried out.

"We preach that God is love, and that's right, of course; but maybe we say it too often—God is also a God of justice." The two-way radio still squawks from beneath the dash. Boet Gilde is committed to the tradition of the CRC; he is conservative and forceful. He believes that one role of the church is evangelism, but that the primary role is still ministering to the needs of its own. "Evangelism! Evangelism! People are always talking about evangelism. But in our tradition the worship service, the sermon, comes first. Our first responsibility is to our own people."

His argument is interrupted by the radio. He makes a U-turn in the middle of the street and heads south on the Dixie Highway, back about a mile or so to a place where a man lies on the pavement in a puddle of blood. He pulls up in front of a bar—Mickey's Tap—and steps out of the car with his nightstick/flashlight. He walks into the middle of the crowd.

The man on the ground, already drunk, had been seen by a biker carrying liquor out of a bar already closed for the night. It is after four in the morning. Somehow, the prone man had pushed his hand through the front window of an adjoining business, severing some veins. In the dim light overhead, the blood seems purple against the blacktop. It spots his "old lady's" shoes. She hovers over him and he swears at her. He is arrested for burglary, for lifting three, maybe four cases of beer from a sleazy bar. A squad take him to the hospital.

When the bar owner comes, he, too, is drunk. The air is as thick with vulgarity as it is with the cloying smell of liquor. The owner stumbles into his place and checks his loss. When he comes out, he swears at the burglar's old lady because, it seems, he knows her and the thief. Boet Gilde has to deal with this mess; the rest of us are sleeping, somewhere out there in safety, far removed from the "obdurate in heart and will."

We are all depraved, we confess. But Boet Gilde smells depravity, he hears it, he sees it nightly, graphically. It threatens him with rocks and bottles and hollow-head bullets that can rip off an arm. Boet Gilde has very decided notions about things—about criminals and courts. We are often admonished to understand the criminal; we might allow ourselves some time to understand our police as well.

"People see the negative aspect of police work. They don't see us give a bum a Burger King hamburger," he says. When we consider his opinions, we might remember that most of us never see a bum at all.

20

Al Kraker and Bev Kole

Wednesday was a big day for Al Kraker. To the east, Lake Michigan growled in thick, gray clouds, as it often does in February, and to the north and south, the wind staggered the smoke from the stacks of Milwaukee's industrial skyline. Outside the fourth-floor lab on the campus of the University of Wisconsin-Milwaukee, the city looked dirty and uninviting, the weather miserable—damp and cold, the kind of weather that sets folks from the upper Midwest scampering for the balmy promises of the sunbelt.

But in another world altogether, Wednesday was a big day. For four years of graduate research, much of Al Kraker's study and attention has focused on a different world, a world that nearly all of the suburban commuters who choke the city's early morning access routes never see, despite the fact that this other world, too often unknown, may be the most fundamental world in their lives.

Al Kraker is a biochemist, and the world he watches, while sequestered in the university lab, is the world within us, within all of us, the world of proteins and elements and enzymes, the chemical world of our bodies, a world made accessible only by the most incredibly scientific hardware, computers specifically designed to measure and examine component parts of our body chemistry, then print out wide sheets full of facts and digits that Al Kraker reads as leisurely as the morning paper. This inner world is fully as real as the smokestack skyline, of course, but our collective ignorance of it stamps us all provincial, even the most cosmopolitan among us.

And Wednesday was a big day, because on Wednesday Al Kraker discovered a specific protein—metallothionein—in a fluid tumor taken from a laboratory mouse with pink eyes. Reading those results on a computer printout made Wednesday a big day.

In Milwaukee, maybe a hundred people became parents on that same Wednesday. Somewhere in the city a builder finished a condominium, a fourth grader learned to multiply, a realtor sold a house, a factory worker was laid off. Yet, Al Kraker believes that his discovery of this protein's presence in a mouse tumor tissue made this February Wednesday as big a day for each of us as those other more immediate concerns did for the persons involved. For Al Kraker, living is a blessing made possible by the interplay of chemicals that finally determine definitions for physical life and death.

"It's not easy for a 'non-science' person to understand how extraordinarily complex something as common as a body is. You take things for granted," he says. "People have babies, babies grow up, and things go on. But just the fact that a youngster comes into being! The amount of biochemistry that occurs. . . And very little is really known why one cell becomes an eye and another a fingernail, and the fact that all of this has been worked out and been functioning for years is an indication and a testimony of God's power and majesty."

When Al Kraker outlines his research on a blackboard, up there at the top, the goal of his study—and his enemy—is cancer. Few words in our language strike such immediate terror as *cancer*. We use it as a metaphor to mean malignant rottenness—"a cancer in

165

the White House," said presidential adviser John Dean several years ago. And our metaphoric use of the word is apt, for cancer is the inordinate, uncontrollable death of our body's component part, its cells. Most of us define cancer with connotative images: damp handkerchiefs, withered bodies, and seemingly endless hospital visits—physical pain, mental anguish, and even spiritual depression. In our minds cancer means, all too horrifyingly often, a diagnosis that sets one upon an inexorable march to gravesite interment.

Biochemists like Al Kraker won't change basic definitions, but they do seek to shake loose the horrid connotations of a word like *cancer*. The process is as hard and long as it is detailed. The protein in the tumor of a mouse is one fragment of the useful knowledge required to understand, and thereby to treat, cancerous cells. On Wednesday, when Al found a specific protein in a new tumor, he fit another piece into an immense picture puzzle. But he can't use the top of the box to piece things together properly because there is no model. Science can make guesses, of course; and Al Kraker knows what he thinks part of the picture looks like, but right now the outcome of all the research is known only to the Great Designer.

Cancer research, like much of today's scientific inquiry, is, by structure, elitist; few of those many commuters on Milwaukee's freeways have the ability, perhaps, to comprehend the chemical miracles Al watches in his fourth-floor lab. But because few of our lives have been left untouched by cancer's effects, we might try to understand the nature of Al's work. We know that many of the elements of the periodic table exist within the human body—some, like sodium, phosphorous, chlorine, for example, in much greater quantities than others, like silicon, nickel, or zinc. These lesser elements, known as trace elements, are necessary for life and health despite their limited quantities. In other words, we need zinc within us, even though the amount of that element cannot be measured in any quantity so bulky as ounces. What Al knows is that in the cells of the body this trace of zinc piggybacks on a protein called metallothionein. Where one finds this protein, one finds zinc. Finding that protein in a different tumor from the one they had been working with for several years suggests to Al that zinc itself is necessary for the growth of any tumor.

Therefore, Al has good cause to believe that shutting off the supply of life-bringing zinc to a tumor would be the same as cutting off this tumor's growth. But he knows that simply curtailing zinc would trigger other horrid effects in a mouse with a tumor, or in a human being with a tumor. So what must be understood is how to control the amount of zinc getting to a tumor without depriving the rest of the cell of necessary zinc. Therefore, what his research seeks to accomplish is to characterize what happens to the zinc as it is carried into the cell by the protein metallothionein—to be able to say exactly where the zinc gets unloaded and why—because knowledge is prerequisite to cure. If scientists know why and how zinc moves from its protein carrier in the tumor cells, then, maybe, they can in some manner deny the tumor its zinc and stop its growth, without affecting the rest of the organism. Shut off the tumor's growth and you can control cancer, and the control of cancer is created when the host of puzzle pieces are finally interlocked.

If a cure for cancer ever comes, one can speculate that it will originate from some laboratory like Al Kraker's. We can be thankful that some of us, blessed with scientific aptitude, are willing to devote our lives to this incredible chemical world within us. But lest we assume Al Kraker's days begin and end on the fourth floor of a university chemistry building, we need only be told that in August Al Kraker—26, Calvin grad, native of Allendale, Michigan, grandson of rural barn-builders, tall, dark-haired—will marry Bev Kole—26,

Bev and Al:
watching and waiting and marrying.

another Calvin grad, also dark-haired, a brown-eyed Christian school teacher, born and reared in Fremont, Michigan.

They met in church—the Brookfield (Wisconsin) Christian Reformed Church—when some cupid-ish usher dropped Al nearly in Bev's lap on the first Sunday night Al attended services there. "Being the kind of person I am," Bev says, unapologetically, "I asked him where he was from."

Al smiles, partly at Bev's highly suspect forwardness, partly out of embarrassment.

"It took him nearly a year to ask me out," Bev says, mocking him.

Today, as I write this, their marriage is only five months away, so when she turns accusing eyes at him, Al feels prodded into some rationalization of his sluggishness. "We had this group at church," he says, "Bev and her roommate and several others," mostly Calvin graduates, students, and professionals in the city. "I was reluctant," he says. "I thought she was nice and had a pleasant personality"—the irony sticks to the deadpan tone of a suddenly very detached scientist. "But I could see that it might cause some problems in this group. I was new and I wasn't sure whose turf I would be infringing upon...."

Their relationship crept up, over, and down through a year of peaks and valleys. "I prayed that God would show me which way to go," Bev says. "I wasn't sure what Al wanted, and I was kind of frustrated in regard to my own Christian life—you know, you're in a Christian school all day long, but sometimes you get to feeling that you're not having much effect."

And that's when something happened to tangle their lives together. Bev noticed a thickening on her leg. A doctor recommended having it removed—a "fatty tumor," he called it. And when the operation was completed, an operation everyone insisted would be routine, the tumor they took out was found to be malignant. Al's blackboard enemy—the target of four years of basic research in mice and proteins and zinc—onerous cancer, snuck into their lives, totally unforeseen.

"After the tumor, everything changed," Bev says. "I think there's a connection between the tumor and the way things worked out." When she says it, she measures her own convictions by her fiancé's eyes, the eyes of a scientist, maybe a shade less willing to ascribe chemical reactions to God's answers to prayer.

They remember that day well. "We were going out steadily at the time," Al says. I went to the hospital with her. Her doctor told me he wanted to talk to me in the hall, and he told me that he thought the tumor was malignant. I had no idea. I was crushed. I remember leaning up against the wall. And he just walked away and let me stand there against the wall. So I called Bev's parents and told them, and then told Bev...."

Bev remembers Al coming into the room. "They had scratched my eye somehow—the anesthesiologist—and whenever I would open my eye, it would burn. I was upset. While this eye thing was going on, he came in and told me that the tumor was maybe malignant."

Four years of research at Blodgett Memorial Hospital in Grand Rapids, Michigan, plus four more years of cancer research made Al well acquainted with both medical treatment and hospital ritual, and he is somewhat critical of the business of medicine. "Bev's doctor called her up on the phone to verify the fact that it was malignant. He didn't ask her to come in and talk or anything—just told her over the phone! I was livid!"

The malignancy of the original tumor demanded additional hospitalization for Bev. Through successive surgeries the people of the church and school community, Bev says, were "caring, concerned, sensitive—always willing to help." "They were a real comfort," Al adds.

Surgery, radiation, chemotherapy: cancer treatment

is packaged in familiar language to us. First, in order to eliminate the tumor itself, Bev submitted to surgery. Then, radiation therapy for seven weeks. "You go in early in the morning, every morning, get lined up—you don't feel a thing until later." Sometimes the hardware can be frightening: "There's this fantastic machine above you, and you're lying there and they tell you, 'It's going to sound like an airplane—maybe you'd better hold your ears.' Then everybody leaves the room through a door this thick—it's huge! They watch you on a little television screen. And there you are, all by yourself. It's kind of scary."

Chemotherapy is less of a treat. Poisons used in chemotherapy destroy malignant cells that may have moved from the tumor into other areas of the body. But the body's chemistry reacts violently—long bouts of nausea. "Actually, the monthly treatments get progressively worse," Al says. "In addition to the regular physiological responses, there are psychological aspects involved." The memory of the last treatment infects the anticipation of the next.

Bev has had chemotherapy for almost a year already, and the treatments have not been easy. "It took ten or eleven times before they had the right combination worked out," Al says. "The three drugs given for chemotherapy do not vary, but there are other anti-nausea drugs given that must be regulated, based on the patient's reaction."

The chemotherapy is torturous for both Bev and Al. Bev drives directly from the school to the hospital on Thursday afternoons, undergoes the same ritual of tests and preparations, and receives the IVs by about nine at night. She sleeps very little—the nurses' frequent tests, the initial nausea, the anticipation of tomorrow's ordeal of sickness keep rest down to infrequent slips in and out of consciousness.

Friday morning the drugs go in. Al is back at her side. "I'll tell you what he does," she says. "He sits

171

next to me when I'm lying in bed, and whenever I get sick—it goes from every ten minutes to once every half hour—he helps me up and then tucks me back in when I lie back down, keeping me warm. I'm really out of it—we don't talk at all." It goes on all day long and into Friday night.

By late Friday night the battle stops, and by Saturday she can go home and rest. By Saturday night she can eat a little, and by Sunday, she's starting to feel better. On Monday she makes a big meal for lunch, her first meal, and Al comes over.

Ironically, today the chemotherapy—the treatment—is the most painful aspect of the problem. But Bev claims never to have allowed herself to feel down about the malignancy. "I personally feel that God is in control. I don't have a real negative view—like I think I'm going to die next year, nothing like that. I just don't feel like it's the end. Maybe it's because I've already seen God work in people through me. So I know the power that's there."

Meanwhile, life goes on, and Al and Bev prepare for an August 14 wedding in Grand Rapids, the reception at Calvin—a big wedding, lots of attendants. Like every other chemotherapy patient, Bev lost much of her hair when the treatments began. By August she hopes to box the wig she bought months ago and wear her own hair. Al reminds her that right now, beneath the wig, she looks like a punk rock star.

And then they'll watch for signs in the next two years, the critical years. If there's nothing in five years, things will be looking good; if ten years pass without problems, the doctors say the cancer likely won't be back.

Many of us know that ten years of marriage isn't a long time, but in ten years cancer research could create a whole new era, given the progress already being made and the advances in technology. Meanwhile, four floors up above a university campus, Al Kraker will continue watching the zinc on metallothionein protein, plotting its every move, hoping that he can get it right, hoping that he can say he knows exactly what happens in a microscopic world that seems to the rest of us more fiction than fact.

Zinc is his tiny picture of the big puzzle, his little part in the greater cancer hypothesis, and if he can get his part right, success will come so much sweeter.

Today there is a face in every computer printout he reads. He can't leave his work at the office because Bev is there with him. And that's why Wednesday was a big day for Al Kraker.

21

Canadian Oil, Saudi Arabia, and Bill Oostenbrink

When Bill Oostenbrink picked up his newspaper on Thursday, April 23, 1981, two front-page headlines blurted out big breaking stories. First, the National Energy Board of Canada had approved Interprovincial Pipe Line Limited's request to construct a $400-million oil pipeline connecting northern Mackenzie Valley oilfields with existing pipelines in northern Alberta. The approval came despite the strident pleas of the Native Canadian tribe officials, one of whom was quoted as calling the decision "programming genocide."

The second story reported how the Sundance Oil Company of Calgary, Alberta, had located a "super giant" oil-field ninety kilometers southwest of Edmonton, a find one geologist guessed would be the third largest in western Canada.

An economist for Mobil Oil, Bill Oostenbrink is a troubleshooter of sorts, even though he rarely gets close to the derricks or refineries that one finds everywhere in Alberta, from the low plain farms of the old Ukranian immigrants to the foothill cattle kingdoms that skirt the Rockies. Today, oil is the lifeblood of Albertan economics, and Calgary and Edmonton, the twin cities of the province, are boomtowns, anomalies in the pattern of economic stagnation and atrophy that characterizes most of the cities of the continent.

Calgary stretches its youthful suburbs and developments out over the rolling hills, the snow-covered Rockies standing like a backdrop to the west. If Montreal and Ottawa, and New York and Pittsburgh are city senior citizens, Calgary is a brash adolescent, its streets charged with traffic, its outskirts almost daily shoving themselves further into the rangeland, its downtown still young enough to avoid obsolescence. Calgary is like Denver or Dallas in the States—rich, young, muscular, a modern western city.

Something close to a million dollars a day accrues in the province's pocketbook, surplus money labeled a "heritage fund." Today, when so many provinces and states pinch for every nickel of revenue, Alberta worries about how to spend its capital. And it's all because of oil.

The process commences with geologists, who read clues in rocks and valleys and make educated guesses at the kinds of formations that lie thousands of feet below the earth's surface. Then geophysicists take over and drive vibrator trucks over areas of high potential, bouncing seismic waves off subsurface rock layers, creating tiny earthquakes which, when read, become the source of a seismic map, a very detailed picture of the geometry of subsurface formations.

The "roughnecks" come next, ablebodied specialists who haul drill rigs, derricks, and diesel engines into areas where the specialists claim ample deposits of oil or gas may exist. The roughnecks poke into the earth with long drills, tipped with heavy bits that look like medieval armaments. When a hole appears productive, cement casings are poured into the shaft to withstand the pressure of the deposit, valves and gauges are installed at the top, and all that remains from the entire process will be an above-ground wellhead or the hammerlike pump jack.

Whatever the well draws—oil or gas—a pipeline is needed to send the deposit to the refinery or processing plant. Southwest of Calgary, the Jumping Pound Gas Plant, one such operation, collects the raw gas from connecting pipes and strips the sour gas of its impurities—sulfur, propane, butane, all of which are themselves marketable commodities. Farmers from Saskatchewan to Missouri use the sulfur in crop fertilizer.

It is an impressive, costly process. From the road crews to the Ph.D.s, from the roughnecks to the gas pump attendants, big oil spends big money and makes big money.

But the effects of oil production can be, of course, devastating. If capital growth is the sole criterion for determining progress, then oil keys such success, but whenever significant change occurs in any culture, something is gained and something is lost. To the native people of northern Alberta, the new pipeline means genocide, the end of a people, the end of their culture. Bill Oostenbrink's job as a troubleshooter is to estimate the kinds of economic and social changes that might occur when Mobil locates a new field. It's his job to minimize the fears of those who see instantaneous wealth as a force of evil. Recently, he spent weeks in Newfoundland, first analyzing the possible effects of a new oilfield development on a fishing village, then reassuring the fisher who fears that new jobs, new people, new money will threaten his or her settled way of life in a seacoast town.

Bill Oostenbrink does economic and social impact studies, then fights two forces: the people whose devotion to a traditional way of life is tempered somewhat by their sense of unforeseen economic gain; and the industrialist whose quest for development and production of petroleum has been muted by a growing sense of intangible values in any culture. "What we try to avoid at all costs," he says, "are the boom-bust syndromes," the night-to-day changes within an economy and a society, the changes that pipelines and refineries

Bill and Marion Oostenbrink:
"infidels" for two and a half years.

and drill rigs can bring in the time it takes you to fill a gas tank.

In order to do his job well, Bill Oostenbrink has to be the Renaissance man of the oil industry; he must know a little about everything, from search to production to marketing. Because of his expertise, Bill, and his wife, Marion, and son Marcel, spent the last two and one-half years in Saudi Arabia, where Bill acted as a consultant for ARAMCO, the Arab-American oil company. They lived on the Persian Gulf in a kind of American conclave in the city of Dhahran. Bill spent his working days pouring over economic tables and oil production estimates and analyzing political maneuverings, trying to create an energy scenario for the future of ARAMCO, a reasonable vision of energy usage and demand in the coming decades.

Living in Saudi Arabia was in some ways a refreshing change for the Oostenbrinks. Marion's face still glows when she reminisces. It was an easy time; there were few commitments to organizations, lots of travel, a new, strange world of mosques and black veils and quaint shops. Bill calls their stay his "sabbatical," implying that his Saudi job gave him some rest, some shirt-sleeve work, and nice long noon hours. On a temporary leave from commitments to church and school, the Oostenbrinks enjoyed their stay in the desert, and yet returned with a warm appreciation for their Christian way of life in Calgary.

Not that there were no annoyances. All imported media were censored, from articles or statements thought unbecoming to the Arab world, to skimpy swimsuits or lingerie ads thought unbecoming to the sanctity of womanhood. They soon tired of black felt-tip deletions and entire pages ripped from news magazines. In two years the Oostenbrinks saw nary a TV kiss, not even the sweet maternal pecks, which were blacked out by some unseen Muslim purist busily protecting his country's moral character from Western decadence. No alcohol. No driving for Marion—a woman's place certainly is not behind the wheel of an automobile.

When Bill explains the Saudi life and the world of Islam, he is precise and analytic, diagramming the basic distinctions—religious, cultural, and geographic—that exist among the Muslim peoples. He speaks with his hands, and he measures his words closely, as if he were following a chart set firmly in his mind. He has a natural authoritative air, and he is convincing, even in light conversation.

"Because of the Kuyperian life view," he says, "I could understand the Saudis better than other Westerners. They have an integrated lifestyle, really; the Koran is the basis for economics, law, and politics." While other Westerners seemed mystified by such a mixture of faith and life, Bill says it seemed perfectly understandable to him.

But the oddest thing about living in an Islamic culture, they say, is being thought of as heathen. "Westerners, and Christians especially, normally think of their own culture as superior to all others, and in a lot of places you can kind of get away with that," he says. "But in a Muslim world, you are the infidels." Westerners, in fact, cannot be buried in Saudi Arabia, and the Oostenbrinks could not have gone to a mosque even if they had desired to. To the Saudis, Christians are deviants.

"Religion is a strong force in their lives, but it doesn't shape their living, really. It's religion by prescription—certain forms of behavior are expected, and once these are fulfilled, one is assured of heaven," Bill says.

Marion had to grow accustomed to shopping in the Arab world. No matter how interested she might have been in a length of material, at three the shopkeeper would send her out of the shop, telling her he had to go upstairs to pray. The entire city would shut down at

Big oil:
spending and making big money.

prayer time, she says—doors locked, window blinds dropped, the practice of faith very much institution-alized.

"Too often we institutionalize things in our church," she says. "We have meetings to set up meetings." Perhaps it is something their slow-paced Saudi sojourn taught them. "In the CRC we do things by institution, not by personal association, and I'm sure that the personal way is more effective in winning over people," Bill says. They have experienced the extreme of institutional religion; no Muslim even thinks of talking religion to someone he or she simply considers to be heathen.

And yet, according to the Oostenbrinks, the institutions are the church's strength. Marion calls it "outreach"—Christian labor, politics, education—and says the CRC takes on significant responsibility in the secular world. And Bill calls it the "world and life view" of the CRC, strong biblical principles integrated into all areas of life. Ironically, perhaps, it is the same kind of approach they witnessed firsthand in Dhahran.

The Oostenbrink home is a museum of their travels. They sit on chairs from Norway, Saudi coffee pots knick-knack the Oriental buffet, and, of course, a little Dutch maiden in traditional dress sits near the fireplace. They live in an established suburb of Calgary, near a reservoir of city water, left dangerously low from the mild winter.

Dwindling resources, like water, concern Bill Oostenbrink, as both a professional and a Christian. We would do well to listen to him; the Arabs have. "It's very important to recognize that the basic forms of energy—gas and oil—are limited," he says in his own serious manner. "Given this situation, we need to husband our resources, stretch them out, and then gradually move toward the more renewable sources like solar energy." But presently, he says, even the most advanced forms of solar energy are five times more expensive than oil or gas.

"We cannot just look into the next few years; before we know it, 1990 will be upon us—and we are still using energy at an alarming rate. The US is using three billion barrels of oil per year, and it has reserves for only ten years. We may find more reserves, but the big, easy ones are gone. We are now down to rabbit hunting in the industry." He speaks carefully.

"We must think of the next generations. In the entire world, the oil reserves are adequate for only about twenty-five years. We'll need to restructure the whole industrial world.

"Today we're stuck with high unemployment because a decade ago no one believed there was a shortage. That was before 1973, the oil embargo, and the dramatic increase in oil prices. Now we know."

Those are hard words, and in Alberta those words seem needlessly pessimistic. In Calgary the streets are full of growth, the suburbs burgeoning, oil revenue multiplying incredibly quickly. But Bill Oostenbrink knows because it's his job to know, his calling to know. And it's our job, our calling, to listen.

22

Fred Nykamp/Charles Lynn:
A Search for Identity

[*All the names in this story have been changed.*]

Fred Nykamp has an identity problem, and it doesn't take an analyst to recognize it. His problem is a fact of his existence. He was adopted. Fred Nykamp has suffered what some call the ultimate rejection: abandonment by a parent. And he has been presented the greatest gift: food, clothing, shelter—life itself—by a man and women who wanted him in spite of the fact that he wasn't their own.

Maybe he shouldn't have an identity problem. His two sets of parents appear antithetical—villainous natural parents and angelic adoptive parents. But nothing is quite that simple. In Fred Nykamp, one of the timeless debates is personified: the battle between the powers of environment and heredity. His adoptive parents gave him a Dutch, Christian Reformed environment; his natural parents gave him hair color, body shape, the length of his toes. Somewhere between those extremes lies a gallery of personal characteristics —disposition, reactions, emotions—that cannot be as specifically traced as his blue eyes or his religious affiliation. Fred Nykamp knows that part of him isn't Fred Nykamp. Fred Nykamp wanted badly to meet his parents, his blood parents, and therein lies part of his story.

When the work is once begun,
Never leave it till it's done;
Be the labor great or small,
Do it well or not at all.

It is a favorite poem of his mother's. For his parents' anniversary, Fred's wife, Ellen, made it into a stitchery, had it framed, and presented it as a gift. It was appreciated because the poem is a ruling dictum in the lives of Fred's parents.

Fred Nykamp was reared on a farm in rural Michigan. His parents are strict CRC—no drinking, no theater, no bikes on the Sabbath. He was reared in a home in which diligence was thought next to godliness, in which the righteousness of hard work was believed to be holiness in vocation. To Mom and Dad Nykamp, as to many of us, *calling* means bending down and jerking out the stubborn weeds of Adam's curse.

All of the rituals of the CRC were duly observed. As a family, they would arrive early at church, wait in the car for a few minutes, then walk in and sit in the same bench, every morning and evening of every Sunday of every month. The family altar was an institution: two memorized prayers and a psalm read. Many of us know his parents; perhaps they are stereotypical. They make fine caricature, but we know them because they exist among us in good numbers. Some of us see them as stiff; others, as backbone. To some they are rigid; to others, firmly committed.

They never told Fred he was adopted, maybe because telling him would have forced them into an intimacy they never felt comfortable in. He heard about it first when he was nineteen, by accident, while he was visiting an aunt. A neighbor dropped in for coffee. "You don't look like a Nykamp," she said. "That's because he's adopted," his aunt explained. Fred said nothing for the rest of the night.

"I had never dreamed I could have been adopted," he remembers, "but right away I started seeing that things made sense. I always had the feeling I didn't fit. Maybe this was why."

"He went back to his aunt the next morning, asking for more information, but she couldn't say much because the adoption was not talked about. All she remembered was that Grandpa had had an objection about baptism.

"My aunt said she just shook all night," he says. She knew she had revealed something, and she knew her family would disapprove. "The family doesn't always get along well," he says. "She was afraid."

For years the fact of his adoption stayed in him like some latent disease. Often Ellen would badger him about it—"Don't you want to know?" she would ask.

Then, in 1971, sixteen years after his aunt's mistake, he approached his adoptive parents, asking them for a special meeting in a motel room where they were staying while attending a wedding. "They didn't want to talk about it," he says; "they were simply unwilling to share anything." The meeting he had anticipated lasted just a few minutes.

"I remember my aunt telling me, reminding me that my parents got me because they wanted me. That thought stayed in my head." Out of deference or respect or love, he didn't push them for more information.

Fred Nykamp is a tall man. He has light hair, curly hair that falls over his forehead. He takes out an attaché case, snaps it open, points at the contents. The attaché is his other identity—full of letters, certificates, pictures. "My name is Charles Lynn," he says, pulling out a birth certificate. There's little emotion in his voice, little variation in tone. But it is a striking voice, distinctive in pitch, like a high-voltage wire.

When she needed a passport, his sister, who is also adopted, asked him to search for her adoption papers since he was employed in a city office. His search for his sister's identity made him interested in his own identity. A quick search told him that his birth certificate was in a neighboring county's records. He immediately requested that his records be sent to his home address.

One day his wife called him at the office. "There's a letter here from Haskins County," she told him. "Can I open it?"

He told her she could. Over the phone he heard the opener slash the envelope.

"It's all here," Ellen told him. "Everything is here."

At that moment he had a name—Charles Lynn—and a birthplace and a mother.

But there is much more to the story. In December 1978, Fred Nykamp took the first step on the ladder of Alcoholics Anonymous. Years before, he had started to drink with business acquaintances, a vodka martini over lunch. His capacity grew in proportion with his desire. He would hold his breath on elevators so as to keep his drinking from others in the community. Soon, it was three-martini lunches as a matter of course. Afternoons became a few hours of wasted effort.

And progressively things got worse. "You reek!" Ellen would say when he came home from work. He started mixing vodka martinis in coffee cups at home. He'd fall asleep on the sofa. But he stayed a "cool drinker," never letting his love for a high disrupt his sense of religious ritual. Fred Nykamp kept taking his family to church; he went to choir, Bible studies.

"I was there in body, but never in spirit," he says. "There was no closeness between God and me. But I had never really felt closeness either."

Eventually he drank alone, at night. His marriage was beginning to crumble; he felt his entire life disintegrating. Ellen started attending meetings at Al Anon without his knowledge for a short time. He asked to speak to her alone one afternoon; he confessed he was having trouble with alcohol. Just the night before, Ellen had been given the telephone number of an Alcoholics Anonymous member. As of that moment, Fred Nykamp stopped drinking; the man he called became his sponsor and friend.

"When I looked up at the Twelve Steps up there on the wall, I saw 'Sin, Salvation, and Service,' " like an echo from an old catechism class. In a sense, his beliefs became his faith; his ritual changed to worship. On December 27, 1978, he quit drinking. He hasn't touched alcohol since. That part of his story, the Lord willing, is over.

But the Alcoholics Anonymous program involves more than simply quitting. "Part of the program says you shouldn't make a major decision for an entire year after you quit," he remembers. He had been uncertain about exactly what he wanted to know about his other name—Charles Lynn. He didn't know whether he wanted to pursue the story.

He received an answer on December 27, 1979, one year to the day after giving up vodka martinis. The original, complete birth certificate arrived, including father's name, birthplace, and the fact that he had a sister. The decision to continue was made for him, he says.

Alone, he drove to a tiny rural town, only a name to help him search for his blood kin. He asked around town about the name. A librarian didn't know his mother, but knew his mother had a sister named Lois, who lived in a nearby town.

"Why are you interested in my sister?" she asked after he had knocked at her back door.

"She played an important role in my life," he said. "She was my mother."

Three days later, Lois wrote him a letter, told him very plainly to stop the search. "If you wish to continue my sister's happiness, just drop everything," the letter said. "And please do not call me or come here anymore."

187

But Lois did tell him of his sister, and that both sister and mother lived in New Mexico. She promised him that she would write her sister, Fred's natural mother, and tell her that her son had come to find her.

There was nothing to do but wait, wait for his natural mother to ask to see him. Four months passed. Still he heard nothing. He decided finally to write her himself, but the letter he wrote, introducing himself as her son, never made it to her.

Two weeks later he received a long-distance call from his sister in New Mexico. "In the middle of the day, out of nowhere, at the office, there was this voice. She told me her name, said she would like to meet me. She said her mother was critically ill in a hospital."

Within a day he was on the plane to New Mexico. He checked into a motel close to the hospital where his mother was dying. He called his new sister, told her he was there in the city.

His sister came to meet him at the motel and took him out to dinner. He remembers the evening well. "We'd just talk and stare," he says. "Talk and stare. 'Isn't a coincidence...,' we'd say. Things seemed somehow to fit between us. It's hard to describe."

But he waited for his sister's approval to see his dying mother. "I was reading a little book titled *God Guides*," he says, describing the hours he spent in the motel alone, waiting. "The book told stories about how missionaries would pray, then sit and wait for a message. I did too. And the only message I received was 'Wait.' "

A day and a half later his sister told him that he could see his mother. "Do it if you have to," she said. The rest of her family knew nothing of his presence at the motel, nothing in fact of his existence.

Earlier he had bought a spray of flowers for her. That night he woke up at four in the morning. He assumed that waking up then meant it was the time for him to go. The nurses at the hospital said it was okay for him to be with her. He took the flowers.

"There were tubes coming out of her all over," he remembers. "She was dying. But I could see the resemblance, and there was this extreme warmth in the room, from the moment I went in. I told her who I was. At first she seemed restless. I had all different emotions in me—regret that I hadn't come to her sooner. . . relief that I'd finally found her."

"I sat there next to her, and she took my hand and held it against herself. The tube from her stomach was almost clear blood. I stayed till eleven. Then I told her I had to leave before the rest of her family came."

"Okay," she said. It was the only word she spoke to him.

She died at four on Monday morning. He had seen his mother for the first time on her last day, on a Sunday, Mother's Day.

Today Fred Nykamp has a natural sister in New Mexico and a Scotch Baptist father he later found in Florida, a man who was unaware of ever having fathered a child. He has a family heirloom watch from his natural father, Fred being the man's only child.

And he has an adoptive family in rural Michigan. He told them by letter about the search, about his natural parents, about his own feelings. They haven't responded. Someday, perhaps, they will talk about it.

Recently he visited a recovering alcoholic in the hospital. It's part of the Alcoholics Anonymous plan and part of his confession—helping.

"I'm sure there's a purpose, a plan, for what's happening in your life," he told her.

The woman looked at him, squinted. "You're a religious person, aren't you?" she asked.

"Yes, I am," he said.

Of that identity he is sure.

23

Harold Aardema:
The Happy Life of an
Outspoken Country Editor

Okay, you modern kids. So you think you know what strict is.

Way, way back in the primitive days of my childhood, back so far sometimes I think I can remember when the dinosaurs ate leaves off the backyard apple tree, way back then, strict was strict.

If you'd ask Harold Aardema his age, likely as not he'd say something like "old enough to know better." He's a broad-shouldered man; his thick biceps pack the sleeves of the sweatsuit he wears when he takes his morning constitutional up and down the sidewalks of his favorite town, his native Doon, Iowa. He looks comfortable behind a desk he designed, in a spacious room he designed, in a house he designed a few years back. He doesn't drink and he doesn't smoke, but those who know him best have caught him sneaking a pinch of snuff now and then, guiltily, as if he were caught thinking of girls in church. His hair is thin, but it's long and curly in the back, maybe too long for the editor of the *Doon Press*.

It was strict all the way down the line: the family, the preacher, the teacher, the cop, the judge, the neighbor. The German Lutherans were strict. So were the Irish

Catholics and the Congregationalists. But I think the Dutch Calvinists "outbested" them all. They made even the holy men of the Jewish synagogue look like grandpa teddy bears.

Doon is not a typical Dutch Siouxland village. It sits on a sloping ridge overlooking the Rock River valley and stands on the edge of the big Hollander sanctuary that lies peacefully to the south and east. There are three Reformed churches—Protestant Reformed (PR), Christian Reformed (CR) and Reformed (RC)—and two different Christian schools here in a town of significantly less than a thousand—even on Saturday nights or Sunday mornings. You would surely get an argument on this, but the sociology of Doon is rare: the PRs rank as most holy, then the CRs, then the RCs—all three "outbesting" the others. Doon is a rich town, warm and colorful, abrasive and surprising, wholly more fascinating than the laboratory cleanliness of an Orange City or a Sioux Center. And it suits Doon's Harold Aardema just fine.

My family, I think, was somewhat liberal for its time. Only now do I dare confess that failure. Liberal families then were called "loose." It didn't take much to get that very harsh label, and it was hard to get rid of.

Harold says his family didn't particularly like that characterization—*loose* has connotations of late nights in dark, dingy places. "I'm a fullblooded Frisian, for better or for worse," he says, a wry smile breaking across his face. A member of the PR church from the day of his birth to age twenty-seven, he left, as he explains, with no hard feelings, sure, he says, that good works are a significant part of the Christian life, tired of being cemented in place by an overemphasis on God's sovereignty, and torn by what he says was the constant infighting, the doctrinal dueling of the elect.

191

Harold Aardema:
a loving curmudgeon.

Parents then didn't go in for kissing and hugging much. The prevailing stand was hit 'em and hiss at 'em according to the injunction, "Spare the rod and spoil the child."

Most parents were pretty human though, and didn't really like the brutal stuff, so the injunction got mostly lip service.

And there's that same playful contradiction in Harold Aardema. He sits back in the wheelchair he has occupied since a childhood bout with polio and laughs out loud at the small-town people he deeply loves. "And I love my church. I sometimes sit and look over the people there and my heart fills right up," he says. "But then sometimes I dislike the whole business bad."

These words became very holy: "don't," "you mustn't," "that's worldly," "only the _____ kids do it," "watch out or you'll get burned," "don't."

We lived with that language. Had to. It wasn't so bad Monday through Saturday, but Sundays were something to handle both physically and psychologically. We got a double dose of negative ethic. Sunday was called "the Lord's Day." It was not a fun day in the lives of most Dutch Calvinist kids of that time. Had we known Jesus' retort to the Pharisees, "The sabbath was made for man and not man for the sabbath," after he fractured one of the Sunday work rules . . . but we wouldn't have dared.

In the best families Sunday began already on Saturday night. Mothers peeled the spuds to reduce the work offense, and the holiest fathers shaved on Saturday night, not Sunday morning. Then it was early to bed to prepare for the Lord's Day.

He very much enjoys his role as a kind of loving curmudgeon, poking away at the foibles of an ethno-religious heritage as much a part of his own vision as his eyeglasses. We might call it an all-too-human

193

love/hate affair, this relationship of his, but it never quite reaches the latter extreme.

And all of this comes out weekly in Harold's own mosaic of Siouxland—news, ads, paid propaganda, travel, obituaries, editorials, nostalgia, humor, court records, wedding pictures, and recitals of Sunday visitations—the *Doon Press,* largest paid circulation of any weekly in Northwest Iowa, a kind of legend both inside and outside of its own hog and soybean corner of the state.

The dominies in those days delivered themselves of heavy homilies, weighted on the doctrinal side, weak on the human side, and they delivered these in voice and manner rather different from the nice guy we chanced to meet on the street during the week. The service called for one and a half hours in church. The long prayer and preaching took up most of the time. The sermons were three-pointers that shot three feet over our heads. Time dragged along. Thanks to pocketfuls of peppermints, we survived.

There's nearly as much of this kind of history as there is news in Aardema's *Doon Press.* "The kids are interested," he says, "and the folks love it." A weekly column, "The Good Old Days," is often complemented by the personal contributions of one of Harold's nearly 5,000 readers—letters, anecdotes, memories of life in Siouxland fifty, sixty, even seventy years past—everything from a record of who married whom and when, to a description of sore, cornpicking hands. The truth is, it's Harold who loves history, and his readers get it weekly in his paper (whether or not they like it), spiced energetically, irresistibly, with Harold's own enthusiasm.

Yes, we all survived the long, long Sundays, the long-winded sermons, the many no-nos. We not only survived.

194

We wouldn't have missed it for anything. Some of us are still playing roles and are only conventionally respectable. Some of us have grown.

Harold has. The punchy combination of spoofin' and spittin' and "spottin' " and smilin' verifies that Harold Aardema is by committed choice one of God's people called Christian Reformed. His feistiness, perhaps, is a Frisian inheritance, something passed on; his energetic love for the church, the Lord, and his people, is his by choice, not worn for conventional, small-town respectability.

Serious ethics must be both positive and liberating. Augustine's one-liner perhaps said it best when he enjoined: "Love God and do as you please."

Some might call that line almost antinomian; some might think Harold is rattling sharpened cornstalks in the faces of the Pharisees in Doon or Sioux Center or Grand Rapids. Harold calls it his own brand of personal journalism—it's titled the *Doon Press*. And there isn't another paper in the nation where you're going to read an editorial like that one. If you're interested, write Harold at Doon.

195

24

The Tan Family

Unlike other denominations, when we count noses, we count families. Families are our special pride and joy. A handsome husband, Sunday-suited, his wife, neatly dressed, their two or three or more children, in ascending order, all clean-cut, marching demurely toward an empty front pew—that image fully satisfies, especially when too many churches appear inordinately peopled by women and children or grandparents.

We treasure our families, and we do so on the basis of our own covenantal theology. Ben and Audrey Tan grew up as part of a family, an ethnic Chinese family in Indonesia, where being Chinese meant being afforded minority status, with all the attendant honors of that designation—prejudice, discrimation, outright rejection. In a society where other institutions turn against you, you have little left but family. Ben and Audrey Tan were reared in austere Chinese families, tight, hierarchical circles where the only source for preservation was the vitality and success of the younger generation.

We don't need sociologists to tell us that the family unit in Eastern culture differs drastically from that in the Western one. The Decalogue weekly admonishes us to "honor" our parents, a word perhaps too simply translated as "obey." But in the traditional Eastern family, *honor* has a less moralistic and far more encompassing scope. To honor means more than simply picking up your bedroom or carrying out the garbage when mother asks. Ben and Audrey Tan were reared in Chinese families where children asked no questions of their parents' way of life, for an interrogative sentence presumed some doubt, and doubt was too dangerously close to, nearly synonymous with, dishonor. Honor is a way of living, not a behavior one wears.

Ben and Audrey Tan were reared in Buddhist, Confucianist, Chinese families. When they started attending the Christian church, their parents, their grandparents, their uncles, their aunts, their entire families, saw the move as a most public and dishonoring slap in the face. For the Tans, the decision for Christ was no momentary, emotional swell, but an arduous, fearful, yet fully satisfying commitment that grew from a series of unanswerable questions, and then solidified when grace itself freed them not only from sin, but also from a respected tradition of generations, and gave them both the insight to live as Chinese Christians and the strength to continue to love families who couldn't help but see the change as a most horrible rejection.

"My father became physically sick," Audrey says. "He felt pain; he vomited for three days." Ben remembers the reaction of an uncle, the man who was paying for his university education and buying the clothes Ben wore to class: "He ridiculed Christianity. He threw Bibles around."

"But you must understand that our Christianity was a rejection of heritage," Ben adds. "To them we were becoming Western, and to them Western meant a loss of respect." The Tans' acceptance of the Christian faith was a very physical threat to the older generation; it meant sure rejection in their old age, the loss of their daily bread.

How did it happen? There is no TV evangelist in their spiritual odysseys, not even a missionary with a

197

Audrey and Ben Tan:
believing in the God of Moses.

Chinese Bible. For Ben, it was, first of all, a growing sense of his own inadequacy. Born and reared in Confucian moralism, highly respectful of logic and reason, he began to sense the limitations of his own sense of truth. It happened while he was enrolled at the Institute of Technology at Bandung, while he was living in a boardinghouse with other Chinese students. It happened not in a night but over a period of years. Here, the questions they dared not ask of their parents became the regular stuff of late-night conversations. "What is the purpose of existence?—questions like that began to have meaning. They were sharp questions. And I tried to explain everything logically—that's the way I was brought up."

He started to go to church, almost out of curiosity, an intellectual quest for meaning and purpose. "I knew there was something there, and I wanted to know more." In 1953, during his third year at the institute, he began catechism at the Reformed church, and he found it engaging—faith at its most logical, truth most satisfying. His commitment grew, and in 1955 he was baptized, finally taking the painful, unavoidable step.

For Audrey it was a somewhat different story. Her parents had enrolled her in a Christian school when she was a child because they were convinced of the higher quality of education. Christian school was a beginning, but Christian girl scouts was an even more formative agent. Unlike Ben's family, Audrey's parents were very traditional Buddhists, following the litany of rituals, setting out the special dishes full of food for the honored family dead on the prescribed holy days. She remembers the questions forming in her mind as a child, questions she never dared ask her parents. Her girl scout leader became an accessible adult to a Chinese girl whose mind was burdened with questions. This woman avoided dogmatics when they talked; she simply allowed Audrey's mind the freedom it needed to grow by questions and assertions.

199

"I had an experience," she says today, "and I just hate that word, but I did." It came years later at the end of a turbulent first year at the university, a year full of reading—Zoroaster, Christian Science, the Krishna movement—a year of confusion. Her mind's strength beleaguered by divergent philosophies and conflicting beliefs, she failed her first year's exams.

And then it happened, one day when she and Ben, both scout leaders themselves, were out in a field with the children. Today she nearly blushes to remember it. "I was brought up in math and science," she says. "This was so bizarre, not intellectual at all, but I suddenly had this intense and bright feeling for Christ. I had been completely burdened by worries, frustrations, and troubles. Then this vision: everything was very bright and very simple. I can't explain it; it's not a logical thing." If she could, she would apologize for such a lapse of reason; but the awesome power of the moment, now years past, is too memorable and significant to excuse or forget.

As was university tradition, she was given another chance at the exams, all of them in one day. She passed. In 1954, a year before Ben, she was baptized.

Ben and Audrey's mutual commitment to Christianity placed them in a strange position, somewhat ostracized from their close-knit Chinese families, yet convicted to remain Chinese. Their faith demanded some compromise: the affirmation of faith plus the allegiance to a respected Chinese culture and family.

"You cannot rub the family too much," Audrey says. "You have to accommodate yourselves to their lives." For Ben, accommodation means playing a role in family ritual. Ben follows the others and bows his head at the altar of the honored dead. "But I pray for the family," he says, "not for the dead." He laughs a bit when he thinks of it, as if it were some secret mission taking place directly under the nose of the antagonist. "It needs to be done," he insists. "When they see me, they say, 'He still remembers those people; he will remember us too.' I have to show by example that my commitment makes me care more for them today than I ever did before."

Ben and Audrey Tan were fifth- and seventh-generation Indonesian. They didn't think of themselves as part of Peking or Taiwan; they were more Indonesian than most of us are really American or Canadian. But in Indonesia, the Chinese are too often considered the "Asian Jews," the sharp, business minds who by graft and guile and sheer business acumen achieve power and wealth. Like the Jews, they have been scapegoats, too often blamed for whatever ill the society suffers.

The Tan family left Indonesia in May of 1968—three kids, four suitcases, and enough money to keep them eating for six weeks. Ironically, they had to lie their way out.

"Where are you going?" the government agent asked.

"Singapore, Hong Kong." Ben held his family close, their suitcases at their sides.

"How long?" he said.

"Two weeks."

The man looked up at them. "What purpose?"

"Vacation."

Audrey remembers leaving Jakharta on the plane. "We looked down and saw millions of lights; it seemed strange that anyone would ever miss us." But lying was their only means out, and the decision to leave— based, in good Chinese fashion, on family—was final.

They left because their daughter would come home from school—Christian school—crying, the victim of racial slurs. Audrey, a teacher of organic chemistry at the pre-med school, knew firsthand that the Chinese were the regular victims of Indonesian affirmative action programs. She feared for the future of her children. Ben heard too many ugly accounts of fellow Chinese victimized by the ruling military power, left defenseless in a legal system built on hatred of the Chinese.

In the attempted Communist coup of 1965, they watched the rightwing Muslim government and the Communist insurgents kill hundreds of thousands of Chinese. And when it was over, when they hoped that peace and stability would return, they felt the discrimination worsen, buttressed by the fear that Peking—and all the Indonesian Chinese by association—provided support for the Communist coup.

Today, thirteen years after immigration, the Tans live in a northern suburb of Los Angeles, in a Californian stucco home, lemon trees in the backyard. Ben is self-employed in the export business—technological equipment to Southeast Asia. Audrey spent two years becoming a registered nurse in those hours her three children were in school, and today she is assistant head nurse in the intensive care unit of Northridge Hospital.

Their children have grown. Nina, the oldest, is in her third year at college, an international business major. David spent last year studying halftime at North Hollywood High and halftime at UCLA. He received a scholarship to attend Dartmouth this year and plans to major in math—"pure math," he says. And Peter, the youngest, a junior at North Hollywood, plans on Calvin College in 1982.

A Tan family dinner of sweet-and-sour chicken is spiced with some talk of education and quantum physics, and a touch of goodnatured family ribbing, especially of Peter, the comic book freak, who laughs along.

The living room walls are decorated with Chinese paintings and wall hangings, and on the floor there are two files of record albums—one file shows a symphony, Beethoven maybe, the other, Blondie, the rock star. The Tans are a hybrid mixture of Chinese heritage, of Indonesian culture, of American—Southern Californian—life, but they are still a family, a bright, loving family, part of the larger family of God, and part of his family called Christian Reformed.

In Indonesia less than 5 percent of the populace was Christian. In that kind of world there is little sectarianism, and the hundreds of Protestant fellowships in this country seem strange to the Tans today. Audrey claims she is no "dogmatic," but she does find strength in the doctrinal commitment of her church—the Trinity, Christ's resurrection—beliefs more liberal churches have made nonessential. She finds it difficult, however, to understand the fervor generated by the debate of women's roles in the church; she hopes for a greater role for women.

Ben finds strength in biblical preaching and in the deep and challenging, intellectually satisfying application of the Word to living, the same quality that drew him to commitment twenty years ago.

Ben chooses his words carefully. He speaks in slowly forming sentences, each word selected, inserted with diligence and purpose. One criticism gathers his ire and pushes his language along. "When we pray," he says, "we are addressing God. And yet some people pray with their bodies sprawled all over." He becomes angry, almost, thinking of it.

It's easy to see why. Ben's commitment, like Audrey's, was no inexpensive change of mind, but a burdensome, yet fulfilling, conviction that this Jehovah God was the one only true God. The Tans have had to pay for their faith; their God is the God of Moses: "I Am Who I Am." Respect, a significant characteristic of his Chinese culture, is not a pose or a gift, but the essential mode of living. Honoring God, to Ben Tan, is more than following a ritual of prayer or keeping the commandments; it is to walk ever humbly, day by day, in the face of the Creator, as a child in the eyes of his Father.

203

25

Margaret De Wit, Calgary, Alberta

There are some who see a human as a machine, a complex of knobs and dials that can function with optimum predictability once strategically programmed. And there are others who see a human as an animal, a parcel of instinctive drives that can be relatively docile once correctly managed by rewards and punishments. We are neither, of course. We are humankind, *Homo sapiens,* God's final creation, an enigmatic parcel of spirit and tissue that defies analogy and metaphor.

But our uniqueness in creation goes even further, for no one is everyone—individually, there are no two of us quite the same. We are the sum total of both our genetic composition and our range of experience, plus more. We are complex, unique.

Margaret De Wit, teacher, traveler, explorer, collector, is as human as each of us, as warm as the best of us, as complex and fascinating as our most enigmatic, a strong woman, yet as fragile as the delicate antiques she keeps like friends in her home.

On Wednesday, Margaret De Wit stood two of her old stained-glass designs in her own front window, ran a two-line ad in the Calgary newspaper, and waited for buyers. When the calls began coming in, she was almost surprised, and when a man whose voice sounded intent promised to stop by and look, Margaret felt more than a little sad.

Margaret De Wit deals in antiques a bit, but let's put that a different way—she occasionally sells collectables. She does not really *deal* them, like some Las Vegas cardsharp, and everything she buys is really a *collectable*—that is, something she has eyes to keep herself. It's just that her collectables start overrunning the modest home in Southwest Calgary, a home she shares with two college students and a huge, gray tomcat she's named Methuselah Felix Sylvestrus: "He adopted me a couple of months ago," she says. When the collectables collect, she feels the need to advertise. So if the man who has promised to come doesn't want the stained glass, there's a part of Margaret that would be much happier in keeping the set. If you can understand that seeming paradox about her, you'll begin to understand her.

If she is, in fact, rich, you certainly wouldn't know it because she does not wear her financial statements. But *things* that show a story to her are important—are dear to her. Her living room is decorated with her treasures. There is a four-foot gravestone rubbing she made herself in England from a 16th-century brass monument, a pious-looking man, palms together. There's a fine little pen-and-ink drawing of "Margaret's House," her old Victorian home in downtown Calgary. There's a ship's lantern from the North Sea; old books from Holland; a 16th-century *insteek ketel*, a copper chimney pot. Her mother's own washtub stand sits on the floor as a footrest. And there's the *schipperke* on her wall, a canal boat's clock from Holland, one of those finely crafted wooden pieces with a nearly exhausted Atlas atop, barely holding up the world on his shoulders, surrounded by two trumpeting angels warning any and all clock-watchers to bide their time here below. Margaret's home has no pretension; it is her personal gallery, and it fits her like a pair of trusted old slippers.

The subdued ticking and pinging chimes of the *schipperke* are as constant in her house as the clock's inherent moralism is to the heritage of Margaret De Wit. "My family were strong church people," she says, "Kuyperian." Her grandfather, Sied De Wit, authored a note on Christian education in the late 1800s, a yellowed document Margaret still has among her collectables, signed by the famous Dutch politician, Groen van Prinsterer. Her father, like her grandfather, was a dry goods merchant in the seacoast city of Harlingen, Friesland, and her mother was a pious woman of character and humor who loved to sing the songs of Moody and Sankey.

Her mother's legacy is no small part of Margaret's life. In 1945, Margaret De Wit, in her teens, grabbed a healthy chunk of cheese from a deserted German army boxcar, just like hundreds of other hungry Hollanders. The Nazis were in full retreat from the Netherlands, too frenzied to pull along all their provisions. She brought it to her mother, more food than the family had seen in five years of occupation. She expected joyful praise.

"Bring it back," her mother told her immediately. To taste the spoils of war was succumbing to anarchy, according to her mother. So Margaret carried the chunk of cheese back to a now-emptied boxcar and laid it there all by itself on the floor, as if it were some kind of strange offering. It was an offering of sorts, a tribute to a kind of austere righteousness that a growing girl, living in a country just freed from five years of enemy occupation, had a difficult job understanding. She remembers the cheese because she has not been able to forget it. To Margaret it is not simply an interesting anecdote; the cheese in the empty boxcar is fraught with meaning, a kind of caricature of her mother—devout, pious, able to discern the spirit of the times and act on the basis of her belief. Such memories become living standards. Lofty standards cut clear lines, perhaps, but do not always make life itself any easier. To understand the pillaged cheese is to begin to understand Margaret De Wit.

Indirectly, it was the war that brought her to Canada in the early 50s. The Canadian soldiers became Frisian heroes, and Canada itself, the land of promise. She worked as a medical secretary for several years following the war, but the lure of a new land, now personified in a sister's life in High River, Alberta, was too strong to withstand, even though, when she arrived in 1954, she thought her trip more of a visit than actual immigration.

At first her work in Alberta was not extremely pleasing—mopping floors and cleaning bedpans in rural hospitals and a sanatorium on the outskirts of Calgary. But soon her professional lot improved; she became a medical secretary again, like she had been in Harlingen. She had a beautiful view of the mountains from the window in her office, she had personal contact with the doctors, and she lived in a lovely old home in Calgary's central city.

Then came hospital renovation. Her job was relocated in the basement, a place she calls "the morgue." She began to dislike it: "ten unhappy women and no windows." There was no contact with doctors, only the chirping voice over Dictaphone tapes. "It was too much," she says. If you know what it's like to work without windows, then perhaps you know how Margaret De Wit felt in "the morgue."

So in her late thirties, on leave of absence from the hospital, she started a first-year course at the University of Calgary. She never returned to her fulltime job, but her summer and parttime work at the hospital helped pay tuition. Five years later she graduated, with honors, with a degree in English, her Calvinist background helping her through Milton's *Paradise Lost*, and her Frisian tongue pulling her with ease through Chaucer's Middle English. She turned down a

Margaret De Wit:
unable to forget the cheese.

teaching assistantship at the university and enrolled instead in education courses, hoping to earn a teaching certificate.

In 1972, she started a brand-new career. One Thursday night she was reading a Dutch newspaper her sister had sent her when she spotted an ad for English teachers in Holland. On Friday she sent a letter asking for more information. On the next Tuesday, a school in The Hague was on the phone, and she had her first teaching job.

"It was like immigrating again," she said. She had left the Netherlands more than twenty years before. She had grown up in Harlingen, but she returned to The Hague, a day-and-night difference in culture. The Reformed church seemed almost unrecognizable: very formal, very liberal. She attended the American church instead, where the congregation was exclusively foreign, more hospitable and caring, used to newcomers. She was happy in Holland; she had a good job, teaching the English language, and the opportunity to travel, to explore Europe. "I'm an explorer," she says, "not a pioneer." But Canada had become home to her—rich, young, free Canada. After two years in The Hague she came back to Calgary.

Nothing lights Margaret's eyes like the telling of the next chapter of her story. She took a job that other educators might describe as a low-prestige position—isolated in a rural, backward, anachronistic community. She was "Teacher" in a Hutterite colony school, sixty miles east of Calgary, on the Alberta high plains. "I loved it there," she says—once, twice, three times at least—and her anecdotes illustrate the fact that the bilingual, Calvinist, immigrant woman was loved reciprocally.

Two of her collectables, items never to be advertised, are icons of the devotion paid her by the Hutterites: a woman's sun (itself almost a symbol of the group) and a spoon with one word etched in the handle

—Teacher. She was a frequent guest at Hutterite homes, and they even suggested that she join them, pointing out that the powers-that-be had already chosen a suitable bachelor for her. She could recite their creeds for them in their own tongue. She understood Anabaptist theology, and, in some ways, she enjoyed their eccentricities. They loved her; she wasn't like other teachers at the school. She understood them, and she loved them.

"It was so interesting," she says. And that's another key phrase to understanding Margaret De Wit. Life itself is interesting to her. Life is one grand curriculum of experience to be discovered, analyzed, appreciated, contemplated, and, at times, suffered. "It was interesting," she says, with the untiring frequency of the *schipperke*'s chimes. All you have to do is scan the book spines in her library to realize the range of her interests: Plato's *Republic, Alberta's High Country,* and *How to Prune Most Anything.*

Today, back in Calgary, she remembers the prairies of the Hutterites with fondness. "I'd stand out there in the open with the prairie cacti in bloom, and I could just feel the Indians all around me. I saw the miracle the dry-land farmers performed every spring. And at night I loved the howl of the coyotes."

And she was fascinated by the Hutterite ways. Because she really wasn't "of them" but was very much "in them," she was able to evaluate their quaint ways at a comfortable distance. "They are really quite fossilized," she says. "They speak a dead German dialect. Many of them don't understand their own theology, and I came to realize that their god is really the machine."

But their festivals charmed her, their drinking schnapps and beer at weddings while singing 16th-century German psalms delighted her, and the rebellious subculture fascinated her. "Whenever you have a powerful authoritarian rule, subcultures flourish like black markets," she says. Sworn pacifists, they hid their beloved hunting rifles from each other. Disdainful of musical instruments, they for some reason allowed their children mouth organs. And somehow radios flourished throughout the colony. "Every spring some of the boys would run away, but almost invariably they would return," she says.

She taught in the one-room school, grades one through nine. She did the administrative work, tested the colony's water quality for the government, and recorded the birds for the Naturalist Society. She was, to them, "Teacher." But when the elders thought she was explaining too much, they reminded her that all the boys really needed to know was how to hammer a nail. Sometimes it was frustrating.

She left after three years, and there are times in every day's activities when she will stop and tell you it was a mistake to leave. It's the sound of children singing: "Are you mine? Yes, I am. All the time? Yes, I am." It's the woman's loving poke on the shoulder when Preacher says right from the pulpit: "*Es ist nicht gut allein zu sein*" ("It is not good that men should be alone," Gen. 2:18). Finally, it is the sense of being very closely attached to a family, while retaining the luxury of being unattached, while holding the freedom to think and feel and act outside of the constraints of that family. Those things she misses.

So this year is her first year teaching sixth grade at the Calgary Christian School, a hybrid descendant of the schools her grandfather had championed in Friesland before the turn of the century. Now she is in a Canadian descendant of her mother's close community. Now she is very much "of the community" and very much "in the community." She sees its strengths and feels its weaknesses in a way she hadn't before, not having been so intimate a part of its continuing development, having spent six days of her week outside the Dutch CRC circle. She, at times, feels alienated, as much today, ironically, as in the past.

Her walls are themselves a testimony to her love of and respect for her religious heritage. To Margaret De Wit, being Reformed means that her confession shapes her view of all things, that her love for the Lord permeates all the areas of God's world. "When we lose that vision," she says, "then we have no reason for separate existence." The strength, the characteristic mark, of the Reformed faith to Margaret De Wit is that world-and-life view. To neglect that, to trade it for anything else, she says, is to give up the name *Reformed*. "At that point we are simply fundamentalists," she says.

Margaret De Wit is unique, and Margaret De Wit is a poet. She has notebooks full of poems, musings, remembrances, story outlines. "Someday I will write," she says, with a fire in her eyes that seems close only to the flame that ignites when she remembers the Hutterites.

Maybe it's the artist in her that makes her unique. Maybe it's the lovely meandering path of her life. Maybe it's her singleness in a church that counts its members by families. Maybe it's the strength of a familial heritage, of cheese in an empty boxcar. Maybe, finally, it's a tension that belongs to each of us: the individual Christian being forced by confession and plain human need into the larger communion of believers, where others are just as human as he or she is and often fit just as awkwardly. It creates a tension in us, especially in those who, like Margaret De Wit, are touched by their experiences in the way a tightly drawn stringed instrument is touched by its player.

The man who called about the stained glass hasn't come yet, but it really doesn't bother Margaret. She rather likes those pieces, and maybe, if he does come, she'll just decide to keep them anyway.

26

The "Talking Doctor": Daniel Bergsma of North Haledon, New Jersey

"My father's a doctor," Donny Bergsma told his pals one afternoon in the backyard, maybe thirty years ago.

The other boys didn't believe him. They had never seen patients walking up to the house, and Mr. Bergsma never dressed up in white like all the other doctors they had ever seen. "Naaww," they told Donny, "he is not."

Even Donny had to think a bit. "He is too," he told them, chin up.

"Is not," they said.

"What kind of doctor is he then?" they asked.

Donny didn't really know how to answer that. He knew his dad didn't go to a hospital every day. "My dad's not a regular doctor," he said. "My dad's a talking doctor."

Dr. Daniel Bergsma *is* a talking doctor; but then most doctors are, of course. Donny meant what he had quickly deduced. His father didn't wear one of those round, shiny things around his neck, he didn't give those awful shots, and he didn't poke popsicle sticks down little boys' throats. But he did talk about doctoring, and Donny knew his father's work had something to do with all those things that most regular doctors do. In a sense, Donny was right.

The ability to converse may be a characteristic that separates us from the animal world, but it doesn't follow that he who talks most is necessarily the most human or most intelligent or most important. Talk is, as they say, cheap. Dr. Daniel Bergsma is somewhat retired today, but the list of his accomplishments has much less to do with talking than with working.

"I've always felt that it's my God-given duty as a Christian to use the brain I was given and do the best I can with it, instead of sitting around waiting for someone else to act," he says.

But things have settled down a bit for him today. Daniel and Nellie Dorothy Bergsma live in a stately brick home on a tree-lined street in North Haledon, New Jersey. Behind him stands a half-century of titles; the full list is nearly summarized in *Who's Who*. We might lift just a sampling.

A.B. Oberlin; M.D. Yale; M.P.H. Michigan

Dr. Bergsma's academic pedigree is made even more auspicious by the fact that he never attended high school. After eighth grade he went to work as a carpenter, then in a drugstore, then for a bank—as head of a savings department. All the while he took night-school courses in preparation for the state regency exams (the equivalent of a high school diploma), which he passed at nineteen years of age.

"I knew when I went to Oberlin that I wanted to go into medicine," he says, and he knew that medical training meant close to a decade of his life. He also knew Nellie Dorothy Arnold, and the two of them had a sort of unspoken commitment already in 1928, nine full years before they were married.

"We lived in a different age then," Nellie remembers. "You lived in a different way too. You didn't get married and then go to school; you went to school and then got married." She smiles like a schoolgirl might. "Besides, we had letters and the phone. We did all right." Her smile widens into a slightly coy grin.

Nellie Arnold went to normal school (a two-year school for training elementary teachers), then taught

214

third-grade children at New Milford, New Jersey, for seven years. Meanwhile, her husband-to-be pushed through Oberlin and Yale. They were married in 1937, the very day Dr. Daniel Bergsma finished his internship. "We've been married for almost forty-five years," she points out, as if to say their marriage hasn't suffered from the late start. The "talking doctor" leans back in his front-room easy chair and smiles.

Served from Capt. to Col. Med. Corps US Army, 1942–46

Dr. Bergsma wasn't actually drafted; the army surgeon general simply made him an offer he couldn't refuse.

Once the war was underway, inductees were herded through the army's testing rituals. Some failed, of course, including some New Jerseyites who were rejected because of venereal disease. Dr. Bergsma, who was then chief of the Bureau of Venereal Disease Control in New Jersey, worked out a system whereby those who failed the physical because of these conditions could be referred directly to his office for identification and treatment. As soon as their problems were cleared up, he notified the selective service, and the rejects were dropped back into the draft pool.

The army was impressed with Bergsma's work. One day the surgeon general sent two top-level representatives to Dr. Bergsma's office and offered him a commission as captain. He could have turned them down, but if he had, they could have drafted him a day later as a lieutenant. "The general's wish is the general's command by army rules," he says.

He spent the war years in the Eastern Defense Command and then in the Caribbean Defense Command, headquartered in Panama, at first as head of venereal disease control, and later, in charge of all preventable disease. His work merited the Legion of Merit award.

State Commissioner of Health, 1948–59

When the war concluded, he asked for and received

an early release to begin a graduate program in public health at the University of Michigan.

Degree in hand, he became eligible for the new head office created in the New Jersey State Department of Health and assumed the position, State Commissioner of Health, in 1948. For eleven years his office supervised everything from disease in udders of cows at Wisconsin dairies to the quality of water on New Jersey beaches. They investigated radiation-related illness in factory workers and supervised food services in summer camps for kids. For eleven years the "talking doctor" headed the one branch of New Jersey government that could, and occasionally did, operate in all the functions of government—creating policy like the legislature, administering regulations like the executive, and enforcing penalties like the judiciary.

V.P. for Medical Services and Professional Education; March of Dimes Birth Defects Foundation

"I've never looked for a job," he says. It's not a lie, but it may be something of a half-truth. In 1959, the March of Dimes was developing a new image for its newly adopted mission. Because of its discovery of safe and effective polio vaccines, the Foundation found itself out of its original job. Its tremendous successes with polio had created its potential demise.

"The changing March of Dimes was a genuine challenge," Dr. Bergsma admits. "I could stay in the official area of public health for the rest of my life, or look for something new." He took the job, and although he didn't really look for it, he did look to it as a challenge.

A healthy dose of optimism and a firm belief in the power of hard work combine to form part of Bergsma's view of things: "It's always been my experience that we should think things out, no matter what it is, and help to change it if need be." No professional experience tested that belief like this new job.

Polio, a national horror, had been bested. The me-

216

Daniel and Nellie Bergsma:
concerned about changes in the church.

chanics of the old March of Dimes organization were still there—advisory boards, research teams—but the Foundation required new experts in a variety of medical specialties and a new image based upon the newly targeted enemy: birth defects.

The "talking doctor" helped push for changes he felt to be mandatory: a more extensive view of birth defects —not simply those related to the brain and spinal column, but everything; the end of the Foundation's commitment to pay for individual care; and the development of a more complete understanding of the causes for and treatments of birth defects. In essence, Dr. Bergsma, in concert with some others, pushed for expansion of the organization at a time when the potential for financial resources seemed to be waning.

The measure of his success in the venture, perhaps, is scores of huge books full of diagnoses and treatments for hundreds of birth defects, books edited by the "talking doctor" and published by the Foundation.

Birth Defects Compendium, now in second edition, is a series of illustrated volumes. Its pages are replete with photographs of disfigured children and adults. The pictures are not for the squeamish. The "talking doctor" may have no syringe in his briefcase, but the kinds of children pictured in his book are definitely helped because of his concern. His aim is to identify every birth defect, seek its cause, and learn to prevent or reduce its damaging effects.

Clinical Professor of Pediatrics, Tufts University, 1975–

Today, Dr. Daniel Bergsma is retired, in a way. He and his wife sit in their living room, in a gallery of family pictures—children and grandchildren. But the one project that pushes him along is the continuing drive to accumulate and process information on birth defects. Trained as a medical doctor, for years an administrator and educator, Dr. Bergsma has, since semi-retirement, become involved in providing medical data and diagnostic assistance via computers.

From his office at Tufts University, the New England School of Medicine, the "talking doctor" seeks to bank in the miraculous computer everything known about birth defects and make it accessible within a minute to doctors in Europe, Honolulu, or Sioux City, to any hospital with a phone linkup and computer terminal. Once books are bound, they are soon outmoded in the continuing march of medical advances. The promise of the computer memory bank is that it can be made to grow with each advance. It breathes like a living organism, offering diagnoses and treatments for children Dr. Bergsma himself never sees.

Member, Christian Reformed Church

Daniel and Nellie Bergsma were reared in the CRC. They met in their mid-teens on a church-sponsored boat trip to Connecticut in the summer of 1926. The church is very dear to them. They recognize some of the changes that have already occurred—a loosening of the traditional restraints on what were called "worldly amusements," for example—but they are concerned about other changes in this church they have been a part of for so long.

"Maybe it's a little thing," Nellie says, "but I feel sad when I see people dressed inappropriately, not new people but people raised in the church." She hesitates saying it, conscious of the fact that some would call her criticism picayune.

Her husband agrees. "There's some evidence, I believe, that a person who is very casual about himself and his dress may become casual about his work performance and ultimately his religious concerns also. If people have carefully selected clothes for playing tennis, for example, but not for church, then I can't help but ask what their concept of churchgoing is."

Daniel and Nellie Bergsma have lunched with senators and governors; he remembers President Eisenhower well. Such meetings were never casual. They have lived most of their adult lives in good clothes. "And worship, if we believe the Reformed view," he says, "is man meeting with God. How can we be casual about that?" The question is meant to be rhetorical and definitive.

The Bergsmas spent twelve years in a Presbyterian church in Trenton; their experience has shaped their vision of the CRC. "I'm concerned," Dr. Bergsma says, "about signs of spiritual illness: loss of respect for biblical wisdom, sermons that stray from preaching the gospel, decreased church attendance or association with another church family, loss of deeply felt enthusiasm for the great hymns of the church. Sooner or later genuine thanksgiving, generosity toward the church, or contentment diminish and finally disappear."

The Bergsmas are concerned about the advent of women in office because they fear the subsequent abdication of responsibility by men, a progressive phenomenon they noted in their Presbyterian church. "We went the other day to a beautiful Episcopalian church in Boston," Dr. Bergsma remembers. "Wonderful service—beautiful music, liturgy. But there were few people and proportionately almost no men. No family groups. The place reveals the signs of a terminal illness and is going to die."

They are thankful for the church's presence and as protective as grandparents. They are thin-skinned about the wooden-shoe problem. "So many people poke fun of the Dutch business," Nellie says. She glances across the room at the man she calls "Daniel." "I say to my husband, 'I'm very proud of the way I was brought up.'" And her husband agrees. "Why should a culture be deliberately sunk like a ship when there are good things in it? If there are some things bad about it—okay, change it. That's the way we progress. But to deliberately ditch it in the name of some generalization —'we should be something else'—that to me is folly."

Nellie Bergsma settles back in her chair. "I'm satisfied with the way things are. I'm satisfied—content," she says. "Maybe it's because I'm older, trained in a different age, but I'm happy in our church and proud of what it has stood for." Her husband nods, smiles.

By the way, the Bergsmas have a daughter, Claire, who married Dr. Robert F. Ashman, presently at the medical school of the University of Iowa. He is a professor, a teacher, and hence a "talking doctor" himself.

And what of little Donny? He's grown up now, of course; and today he's head of the Department of Ophthalmology at the University of Kentucky at Lexington. Today there are three "talking doctors" in the Bergsma family.

27

Henry and Alice Knapper, Windsor, Ontario

Pictures, some black-and-white, some color, decorate the old pump organ in the living room—lots of pictures, some big portraits, wedding portraits, some little snapshots, some tiny ones sprouting from the frames of the bigger ones. There's close to forty grandchildren now, and already ten great-grandchildren. And if they all aren't up there on the organ, you can bet they will be very soon.

The library has *The Robe* and *Navajo and Zuni for Christ*, a number of things in Dutch, and several Billy Graham books in colorful dust jackets. There's a *Calvinist Contact* on the little end table, and *The Banner*, and the newspaper, and a maroon *Let Youth Praise Him* somewhere between the pictures on the pump organ.

The Knappers call it home. It's an old house in an industrial area of Windsor, Ontario, a Canadian suburb of Detroit, one of those houses with the old-type basement—a low ceiling and maybe a naked light bulb hanging here or there from between the 2 × 12 rafters. Like a dungeon to some maybe, but not to Henry Knapper. One man's dungeon is another man's castle. Henry Knapper's basement workshop is his castle.

Henry Knapper worked twenty years for Henry Ford. He says he worked a lathe in the salvage shop. His castle is proof positive of his claim; it's obvious

Henry Knapper just can't throw things away. Everyone has a basement drawer chock-full of rusty nuts and bolts, but Henry Knapper's whole basement is a private salvage shop. Old steel rings hang from between the rafters, bits of corroded iron and tin are stuck into dark corners, and shards of metal poke out of coverless cigar boxes. And of course there's a lathe in the corner, covered by canvas. "Dust," he says, "is the death of good machinery." He speaks with his back to you because his hands are busy reaching for the switch of the fluorescent light above the workbench.

"What do you think of this?" he says. He pulls out a black bicycle pump and fixes the end of the hose to a nozzle mounted on the frame of some mechanical gizmo. The long fluorescent light finally snaps on. He puts his toe on the pump and shoots air into the little machine. Tiny red wheels turn in perfect silence; cylinders as round as quarters pump up and down. It's a marvelous little engine he's demonstrating. His own design. His own creation. "What do you think?" he says again.

You tell him it's really amazing, really great.

"Ja, pretty good, pretty good," he says. "I made it from scratch, you know," he says. "It takes a very long time for such a thing. It's not easy—all those parts."

So you tell him again that it's a wonderful thing, because the truth is, you've never seen anything quite like it before.

"Ja, ja," he says, "but even an old toolmaker will tell you that there is nothing that is perfect. Oh, no." For a second, his eyes search yours.

He moves quickly in his castle, quickly for a man near eighty, quickly like a child in a room full of his favorite toys. It's not nerves that push his thick machinist's fingers, it's pure excitement, plus a healthy dose of workman's pride—the good kind. He shows you a little red wagon he's made for a new

Henry and Alice Knapper:
the grandparents we all hope to be.

grandson and a tall, thin bird, handcarved from a block of wood, its head and beak pointed heavenward. But it's no slow museum tour he gives you through his basement. Following the retired machinist through his basement castle—around the gray shoulders of the old furnace, down the narrow aisles between the stacks of wood and scrap—keeping track of Henry Knapper in his artist's studio is like trying to collar a thrill.

Some characters need no introduction because they are part of all of our experience. We all know Henry Knapper. If he's not the grandfather you have, he's the grandfather you hope to be someday.

And Mrs. Knapper. She doesn't go along on the basement tour. She has seen it all before, of course, but that's not the only reason she stays upstairs. When you come back up through her tidy kitchen, she explains the basement: "Ja," she says, "when you get old like us, it's good to have something to play with." It's the way she says it that counts, because a nicely hidden apology leaks through her words. The fact is, it's Henry's basement down there—not hers, you understand; and she wants no blame for its condition. She wants you to know that she tolerates the Knapper salvage shop, doesn't love it really, but tolerates it only because she loves the artist-in-residence, the father of her ten children.

"Now, Mr. Schaap, what is it you want to know?" Henry says, leaning back in his easy chair, the one with the wooden armrests and the doily draped over the top. His back is to the organ, and an upright lamp stands to the left over the end table, the one with *Calvinist Contact*.

"We came here in '27. We had two kids—Emma and Bert. We came because it was bad times in Holland. I had studied for teacher, finished three years, and then the bad times.

"We came to Sarnia. We had no place to stay. There was nobody to say welcome then. Not like for the second bunch, who came after the war. Then Vander Vliet was the field man, and he or Vellinga was right on the boat. They set those men at ease—the new families. When we come, no one says boo!

"We stayed first at a hotel. It was already out of business. We were the only ones there. A farmer drove up and asked if I wanted to work shares with him. 'Might as well,' I told him. I had no other job.

"He had a house, but it wasn't finished quite yet. I could look through the boards at the stars at night. The roof was only fixed with tar paper on one side—two rows, ja, eight feet. When it rained, we would run underneath. Hah! Ja.

"The Reverend J. R. Brink came in the early years. He did tremendous work. He slept one night in that house. It was a bad storm that night. 'It is a bad storm,' I yelled to him during the night.

" 'Ja,' he yelled.

"I asked him if he was okay.

" 'Ja,' he said, 'I'm okay.'

"Sunday morning I heard him get up, and all of a sudden I heard him—'Yooohh!'—he yelled. I said to him through the wall, 'What is the matter?' The walls, you know, were so flimsy.

" 'My boot was rained full of water, and I put my foot into it and now I am wet up to my rear end,' he said.

"We laughed, of course. And later he preached to a handful of people. We had services in a house.

"There came a man to that house. He was selling fly toxin. He comes in there and grabs his little gun and shoots around two whole cans of toxin! And the floor is black with flies.

" 'There,' he says, 'you can see that this stuff works.'

"I said to that man, 'Well, what is the sense of buying it? They come just as fast back in!'

"Ma, make some tea; this man is thirsty."

A marvelous little machine
from Henry Knapper's private salvage shop.

"Mr. Schaap, you would like some tea?" Mrs. Knapper says.

You dare not say no.

"Is he telling you now the old things?" she says. "Ja, it is different now, eh? People don't live that way like they did when we came here anymore. We were the first ones here! We didn't know anybody. We stayed there in that old hotel with two little kids at first! I didn't know any English. The worst part is you don't know English."

"Now, Ma, don't butt in so much; then I lose my way of thinking."

"Ach, he talks too much. Mr. Schaap, you would like a cookie too?" She rises and goes back to the kitchen.

"We moved to Windsor. The preacher—Rev. Dykstra —got me a job at Ford. He tells me, 'Henry, you are no farmer.'

"We had church services, and we dwindled down to two or three families—two widows and us. Others moved away to farm—Holland Marsh or Sarnia. But we stayed, and I read many a sermon in the YMCA. Emma played the organ, and one of the boys gathered the collection, usually $1.25, but you could buy three pounds of hamburger for a quarter then too!"

The tea is hot from the china cup. The sugar cookie is imported from Holland.

"Did he tell you yet about after the war? At one time I had twenty-seven people—all Dutchmen, just over— in my house. They were all from the train station. Then my children had had enough! Ja, they had had it! 'Ma,' they said, 'you take in any more and we're leaving,' they told me. Those Dutchmen were lying on the floor and upstairs and all over."

Mr. Knapper takes three sips while he allows his wife to tell a part of the story. He starts again. "People in Detroit—Grosse Pointe Church—they brought clothes and furniture for the new immigrants. You be sure to write that too. Rev. Ouwinga too. He helped us out.

They all did great work. You be sure to write that." He lifts his cup again.

Mrs. Knapper takes her turn. "Those days were different though, eh? My boys would come home from cleaning snow from the sidewalks. They would give me the money. 'Mom, I have a quarter,' they would say. A quarter bought three pounds of hamburger. The boys they remember that to this day."

"It was a blessing in disguise—those days," Henry says. "Ja, today we got our own house here, a pension from Ford, some money in the bank, some old-age pension—what more can you ask? And besides that," he says, "we believe that the much bigger life still lies ahead for us, eh?"

It's just like the tea—you can't say no.

Reminiscence rolls on for another two hours, through a pair of eighty-year lives. And when you finally rise to leave, Henry Knapper pulls down a handcarved bird from a shelf in the front room. "This one is almost now done. Here, feel it. Still there is some bumps on there. What do you think?"

The bird's long, slender body reaches upward gracefully, and its beak points straight toward the heavens. You can't help yourself. "Can I buy it from you?" you ask.

"Jus' take it," he says. "Jus' take it along."

Out the kitchen and through the garden, past the mechanical windmill designed and created from scrap in the basement castle, they walk you to the car.

"Mr. Schaap, you would like some good Canadian tomatoes?" Mrs. Knapper says.

You simply cannot say no.

So you leave, a little handcarved bird packed carefully into your suitcase and a shopping bag half-full of Canadian tomatoes, red-ripe, on the floor of the back seat.

"It's a good car, this Ford," Henry says. He means it as an appraisal, not a question.

You don't need to tell yourself that you made some kind of haul at the Henry Knappers, because you know that Henry's handcarved bird and Alice's peck of tomatoes are really just the frosting on the cake.

And the funny thing is, you catch yourself smiling all the way through Detroit.

28

Charlotte Baldwin's
Guardian Angels

Perhaps we lack a systematic approach to the study of guardian angels. Doctrinally based as we are, we may have overlooked them. Worse, we may simply have left them, along with in-front-of-the-church testimonies and certain obtrusive gifts of the Spirit, to a different denominational tradition. So when these angel things pop into our lives, we either silently offer thanks for their help or note them with a smile, with the same kind of smirking levity we express in quoting some dusty Dutch proverb our grandmothers used to lean on.

Whatever the cause of our neglect, we rarely take guardian angels seriously, maybe because we've seen too many fairy godmothers or wizards or genies in odd-shaped bottles. Guardian angels are just plain too speculative; they're the stuff of Disney or Aesop or maybe the Twilight Zone. They seem out of place in the rigorous strategies of Reformed theology.

But discount them as we may, they seem to exist in a myriad of forms, and at least some of us will swear to their omnipresence. Charlotte Baldwin has seen too many of them to be skeptical. Charlotte Baldwin, mother of twelve, full-blooded Pima, born and reared on a desert reservation in central Arizona, has seen guardian angels in sufficient quantity for all of us, and her story is proof of their presence.

Charlotte Baldwin was reared Presbyterian, strict Presbyterian. Nightly, her father would gather the children together in the home or under some mesquite tree and question them. "What did you do today?" he'd ask them. "Did you do what you were supposed to?" The children would drop their faces. "The things you think are fun may be the devil's things," he'd say. He pushed them. He wanted them to be the best of the Pimas. "I have to teach you the right things," he'd say. "I have to raise you." Charlotte's mother would sit respectfully and nod while her husband spoke to the children.

"You know that people are watching you," he'd say. His face was bronze and deeply lined. By day he was a bricklayer in the heat of the desert. By night he tended the family garden. They were too poor for meat. On Sundays the whole family would follow their aged grandmother to the little church.

It was a long speech her father would give them. "You are going to have rough times," he'd say, "but in forty years you'll remember this. God is over us. You've got to live for him."

Charlotte Baldwin has passed those forty years, and her bricklayer father is buried near Sacaton, Arizona, on the desert reservation. But she remembers, just like her father said she would. Fathers don't make stereotypical guardian angels because they don't look like fairy godmothers. Or maybe because we take them for granted. Charlotte's father was the first of her guardian angels.

At Cook Christian Training School in Phoenix she met someone she thought she loved, another Pima, a fine talker and a favorite student. Her whole family, even aunts and uncles, pitched in to pay for Charlotte's beautiful wedding in the little Presbyterian church. Together, married, they left Arizona for California.

But he started drinking. She had never, not once, seen someone drunk. Still newlyweds, they were thrown out of their apartment. The night of their eviction he took her with him to the bar. She was a Christian; she wouldn't drink.

The bartender noticed her sitting alone at a table, her husband already half-gone. "What are you doing here?" he asked her. "Don't you have a home?"

She told him she had no place else to go.

He called a taxi. "I'll send you to my home," he told her. "My wife will care for you. You don't belong here."

She stayed with them for a week, while her husband drank. The bartender's wife bought her clothes because she had none. She had nothing. Even bartenders make guardian angels.

Just four months married, Charlotte wanted an annulment. She wanted to go home to the reservation. Her husband, sober off and on, worked often enough to earn a trip to Arizona, but the night they were to leave, he picked up some of his friends and headed out to Long Beach—three drunk men and Charlotte. She had no idea where Long Beach was from the central Arizona reservation.

The men kept drinking, and the three of them passed out in the car, two in the back seat, her husband in the driver's seat. She was alone in Long Beach. She opened both back doors, and the two drunks spilled out of either side of the back seat, falling in heaps on the sand. Then she pushed her husband over to the passenger side and started the engine herself.

Charlotte could barely drive a car. She was hundreds of miles from Sacaton. She remembered her father's words: "You get in trouble, just remember God is always with you." She says she prayed so hard, so hard. And then she left, directionless.

She stopped a policeman for directions. "I want to go home to Arizona," she told him.

It was the middle of the night. He checked her gas and looked over the car. He filled up her tank with his

Charlotte Baldwin:
her father's sermons still
play nightly in her memory.

own money, and he brought her to the highway, the main highway.

"Get on this road," he said. "Here's my phone number. If you have any trouble, wherever you are, just call me. I'll send someone from that part of the state to help you out. Just call," he said.

Maybe we don't think of police officers as guardian angels as often as we might.

Charlotte's mother always considered her place to be as a helpmeet, a helpmeet to her husband and a mother to her children. Maybe her mother's attitude explains why Charlotte just couldn't quit her husband, though his chronic drunkenness had destroyed any semblance of a marital bond.

For a time they stayed in Arizona, but soon he wanted to wander back to Chicago, where he had been stationed in the service. But they had no money, and now they had a daughter.

They poked along northward, her husband taking jobs wherever he could find work, Charlotte and the baby living in the back seat of the car. Any money she found went for the baby. In the wide-open Oklahoma plains, penniless, she went three days without food so that her baby would have milk. Finally they stopped at a country store.

"Listen," the storekeeper said, "I live just down the road. We'll put you up. How's that?"

They took baths, changed clothes, slept well in soft, dry beds, ate bacon and eggs for breakfast and hamburgers for lunch.

"I told them I was so thankful," she remembers today. "You know," she told them, "I always trust in God, and he always provides. You are the people he has chosen to provide. Behind all this is God." That's what she told them, the Oklahoma country storekeeper and his wife.

Anyone can be a guardian angel.

More than a year passed before they made it to

Chicago. She and her daughter spent three days on Chicago's Clark Street in the back seat of the car, while her husband drank himself into a stupor with some of his army buddies. They made it, she told herself. They had made it to Chicago.

A police officer took her to the Salvation Army in his squad car. She didn't care if she never saw her husband again, ever. She had a warm bed, clean clothes, a warm shelter for her little Vicky, even if it was only temporary.

Somehow, those uniformed Christmas bellringers seem likely candidates for angelship.

And there were so many others. The welfare department women who gave her the plane ticket back to Arizona when her husband left her for good. And David Baldwin, who paid for her divorce so that he could marry Charlotte and be a real father to her two children. Others too numerous to mention. Strange how these angels come in different forms.

And, in a sense, we, the CRC, have become one. Today, sixteen years after she married David Baldwin, some Baldwin laundry is drying on the ping-pong tables of the Fellowship Hall of the red brick CRC Indian Chapel on the northeast side of Chicago. In March the Baldwin family lost their home and all their belongings, everything. A raging fire left David and Charlotte and eight of the twelve kids with no roof. So today there's a TV and a couch in a Sunday school room of the chapel, and a couple of mattresses are down on the floor of another. And a whole bundle of black-haired kids have called the chapel their home for the past few months. They're looking for an apartment of their own, but it isn't easy for a Pima woman with all those kids.

"You're Indian?" the landlords and landladies ask. "You drink?"

She tells them no, but none believe her.

Today we are her guardian angels, and it's right that we should be. "The Christian Reformed Church has been so generous," she says. "They've given me so much. I lost everything, my home of sixteen years, everything—kids' toys, clothes, birth certificates, everything. But I can always rely on the church. I can always get help from these Christian people. I feel bad because I don't like taking money from anybody, but they give it in Christian love, so I accept it."

Charlotte Baldwin has been a member of the Christian Reformed Church for eight years, but she has been a covenant child from the day she was born. Her father's sermons still play nightly in her memory, and no fire can consume the conviction of her mother's confession. No guardian angel—no police officer, no bartender, no welfare agency, no brick church—has been more important to her life than the legacy of belief, four generations of confessing Pima Christians on the desert reservation near Sacaton, Arizona, the little Presbyterian church. It may be impossible to visualize the covenant as some gloriously arrayed guardian angel, but it has been, nonetheless.

" 'Trust in the Lord with all your heart. In all your ways acknowledge him, and he will direct your paths.' That's what I tell my children," she says today, a lifetime of bumps and bruises behind her. That's what she remembers from her father and mother. And that's what she knows to be true.

29

Notre Dame's
Professor Van Engen

John and Sue Van Engen's house looks like the kind of home a historian would live in. There is a formal dining room set with oak furniture, ornate oak, treasured hand-me-downs from Sue's grandmother. And the place sounds like the kind of home a historian would live in. Screaming TV ads never shatter conversation because there is no TV. And once the four little Van Engen boys hike up to bed, the living room rests on the heavy ticking of an old mantel clock, like the rhythm of the human heart—steady, quiet, even wise.

It's an old house, turn-of-the-century vintage, open staircase, living room fireplace, yards of oak woodwork presently hidden beneath a coat of white paint Sue claims is soon coming off. When they moved in, there was no money for an interior decorator, so John and Sue assembled a living room with the furniture they had collected in their many previous moves, and added a beautiful Baldwin both of them play and scores of old books stacked up in ceiling-high bookcases.

Five years the Van Engens have lived in South Bend, Indiana. Five years John has taught medieval history at Notre Dame University, a secluded fortress of ivy walls and statues and football ghosts that sits off by itself northeast of the city—Notre Dame, perhaps the most famous Catholic university in North America.

"When people say, 'What's a Dutch Calvinist doing at Notre Dame?' I just tell them that I'm trying to convert them all." John Van Engen has a rippling laugh that would be startling if it weren't so honest. But his presence is not so hard to explain. Four years at Calvin, five years of graduate work at UCLA, two years on a fellowship at Germany's University of Heidelberg, his first book to be published this fall at the University of California Press—John Van Engen, of Hull, Iowa, has the credentials Notre Dame sought in a historian, a church historian with a special interest in medieval life. Church history, we might remember, begins long before the day Luther slapped his arguments on the door of the church at Wittenberg.

"We all have a historical understanding—some notion of where we've come from, how things used to be in the good old days, and a sense of how things are going to be in the future. But it's the historian's job to be responsible about that historical feeling in us all. For example, when someone says, 'We want to teach seminary students the way they were taught in the thirties,' it's the historian's job to point out that such a position is plainly shortsighted. If we look at the thirties, we'll find weak profs and poor preachers and fights in the church there too."

The study of history to John Van Engen is a means, not an end in itself. And he made a career choice on that basis. Interested in literature, philosophy, and theology, he was persuaded that history was the most efficient means of drawing together those interests. "History," said Henry Ford, "is bunk." But John Van Engen claims such a view is as blind as it is foolish. "Neglecting history is either dangerous or pathetic. For instance, it's dangerous when kids can't remember not to go into the street, and it's pathetic when old people lose their memory, their sense of place. Without a memory, a sense of history, people become either childish or senile."

But he understands the limitations of history. "A sense of history will not give you clear answers in any dilemma because every new situation we face has its own matrix. But history will give you a sense of direction; it is an important part of a person's understanding of him- or herself."

Applying his beliefs to his own life is an interesting challenge for Van Engen. Today he is vice president of the council of the South Bend CRC. When he speaks of his denomination, respect and concern commingle and calm his rippling laughter. But it wasn't always that way. John Van Engen spent almost eight years outside the church, rebellious, fixed in a kind of intellectual aloofness that began, ironically, at Calvin College. Why the rebellion? And what happened to bring him back again, to make him so passionately Reformed today that he laughs about it himself, laughs as if to cover his embarrassment? History can help us.

But historians turn rigid ideologues the moment they affix one solitary cause to any verifiable effect. What happened to John Van Engen happened to many of us, perhaps, many who, right now as they read his story, can remember a time in their lives when they were sure they would never touch a *Banner* again. And it happened for many reasons.

The late 60s were not tender years in which to grow up. Violence became a political tool, and protest, fashionable. Rebellion—long hair, dope, sexual promiscuity, raised fists—became acceptable means of securing identity. Worse, rebellion became, to some, the *only* acceptable means of securing identity. All across the States, radicalized student bodies barricaded major universities. And to some Dutch Reformed kids, even if they came from Hull or McBain, to stay out of the movements of their own generation was a red-faced acknowledgment of the peculiar isolation of the Dutch Reformed incubator—that provincial set of institutions, hopelessly out-of-date, odd, even embarrassing.

For some young Calvinists, the 60s made rebellion a mandate, whether they matriculated at Calvin or Dordt or Berkeley.

But for John Van Engen there is another, personal reason. His father's death when John was three years old (and the oldest of three children) left his mother the difficult task of rearing a family without a husband, a task which, John says, she accomplished with energy, spirit, and dedication. "My mother is independent. She's had to cut her own path," he says. She was reared in the Reformed church, and in *kolonies* like Hull, one learns the science of prejudice by judging other people—Hollanders all—by the branch of Reformed church they attend on Sunday morning. He says that for years she never really sat back in comfort in the CR church. Often, when he was a boy, they would argue together, John taking the traditional CR lines he'd picked up in school. "So all of that is part of my background, and I think that's a part of me that came through in those years."

One specific incident focused his alienation during his Calvin years. A resident advisor his sophomore year, he left the dorm one Friday night to go to a party in Holland where there was some drinking—"a few beers," he says. Meanwhile, one of the guys on his floor got drunk. He fought to keep the kid in school when the other RAs wanted him thrown out, and he won. Then he resigned his staff position, making very clear why he did—"I was drinking that night myself," he told the dean. His rebellion grew from that point, he says. "Essentially, I stopped going to church. I began to read existentialist literature, and I scheduled my classes to avoid [compulsory] chapel. When I couldn't get out of it my senior year, I purposely sat there and read a novel in protest." He sits back in his chair, inhales. "I don't know if I'm proud of that or not proud of that right now," he says.

And he says it as a historian might: he knows that,

John Van Engen:
a champion of the pietists.

for better or worse, all of that has shaped him into what he is.

"I never became anti-religious. It was more that I just didn't have room for it. It didn't fit in. And it was very hard for Sue. She had been absolutely straight longer than I was, and she hated to go to church alone." Four Los Angeles years without church.

Why did he come back to the church he was reared in? He says it was a very gradual process. It started in Germany, in the State Lutheran Church. "I started going every Sunday. I liked the liturgy and music. I was the only kid at that church—the rest were old people."

And his immersion in history and theology, medieval Catholic theology, helped too. "I think that's what I needed. I don't think that I could have studied Reformation theology because of all the rebellion. It's clear that I came back to an understanding of the Christian faith through ancient theologians and devotional writers, and then from there I began to look at my own heritage."

Perhaps it isn't fashionable to say this, but then fashion is but a pawn to a historical understanding. There's a woman in his story. Sue Wessels Van Engen, often more insistent on holding to the devotional conventions than he, had much to do with her husband's return. Maybe it isn't perseverence of the saints, but then, maybe it is.

And then there's one other reason, one reason that reaches up over the others and tugs them all together. A whole lot of us, maybe even the Van Engens' relatives in northwest Iowa, would chalk his return up to the centerpiece of Reformed theology: the covenant —represented in the exchanged promises of baptism.

When you see him walk across the Notre Dame campus, you can't miss the fact that he's not a fightin' Irishman. He has a long, gangling walk he says he inherited from the Van Engens, his hair is straight and Dutch-blond, and he wears a little blue Hans Brinker cap. But it has affected his vision, being at Notre Dame and having spent countless hours absorbed in medieval devotional writers. He has become something of a champion of the pietists among us. "The pietists," he says, "get bad press in our church because the doctrinalists and the Kuyperians don't look kindly on them—'oh those pietists!'" he sneers in imitation. "The pietists are 80 percent of the church!

"In another context I would vigorously defend the doctrinalists or the Kuyperians, but the point is that today the pietists need attention. By not dealing with those people on their terms, we've opened them up to American evangelicalism—they're not getting what they need from us. We've made a mistake by not cultivating the pietist literature, and there are volumes of it. Church historians always talk about German pietism as a significant movement in the development of Protestantism, but pietism, historically, moves from the Netherlands to Germany. But few historians realize that because few historians read Dutch."

Because he's read Dutch pietist literature, he knows that the history of the church has room for a pietist element, in fact has its roots there. He feels the church has to expand once again to meet the needs of its many members who don't see nuclear disarmament or the plight of the Eskimo as issues of faith in the 80s. "Our leaders, the ones in charge of our church and seminary, have never taken pietism seriously because they have been too busy with doctrine or social issues—and I can appreciate that. But what we lose is a middle ground. For instance, what does personal sanctification mean in the late twentieth century, now that drink and dance and cards are all thought of as being outdated prohibitions? We're really in a quandary on that. The Kuyperians are dealing with sanctification on the widest level—speaking up on the issues. But you can't jump to that level without personal, inner sanctification. You cut the pietist's part out of the church, and the church will fall apart."

Keeping the pietists happy, keeping the doctrinalists calm, and allowing the Kuyperians room to move—accomplishing these goals simultaneously is difficult, but "we need to appreciate a sense of diversity. We need mutually to appreciate the Kuyperians and the pietists, the rural and the urban, and there has to be some give-and-take. We need to generate some sense of how diverse we are."

And how must such change be generated? "It has to come through preaching and teaching. That's absolutely foremost. If preaching isn't strong, if it doesn't have solid content, then we're lost as a church. It's leadership. Our church has to overcome a sort of tribal identity without losing the strengths of that identity. The question is whether in the assimilation process we have not already gone so far that the American evangelical found in us all just can't delight anymore in the doctrinal and devotional heritage that is ours. That's what I fear."

John Van Engen sees the loss of identity, ecclesiastical identity, as one of the big problems of today's church. The history of Calvin College, he says, illustrates it. "For a long time, the idea was to get these Dutch kids to understand something about art and philosophy—and I agree. They took for granted that everyone was saturated with Reformed culture. But I asked a class there once, 'Who knows the name Abraham Kuyper?' and most students didn't know! Under the 4-1-4 curriculum today, students still take at least two theology courses, but they don't necessarily have to take Calvin's *Institutes*. I think that is an abomination; it drives me crazy!

"There has to be a sense of who we are and where we came from. Those things used to come from the community. I learned them in school, but it's not there any longer. And too many people at Calvin simply don't seem to see it, because they are still fighting battles already thirty years old."

If there were less determination in his voice, one might wonder whether his own analysis hadn't wearied him into pessimism. But when he talks about his church, it's very clear he's talking about something he sees full of hope and promise, something he's a committed part of today, almost a decade after the Vietnam War.

"We can too easily get ourselves in a situation where the leadership talks about pacifism and nuclear war and women in office, while the people are going crazy because they don't think that's what the Christian faith is all about. And besides, they never hear any of those men talk about personal faith and personal sanctification. *Nabij God te Zijn [To Be Near unto God]*—you know Kuyper wrote as much devotional stuff as he did cultural, and this intensely inner way was the basis of his strength.

"The strength of the CRC is its strong rootedness in a Christian tradition, a strong sense of community that sees the Christian faith as a commitment not only to God but to one another over time. We need to cultivate a sense of who we are in the larger community of Protestant evangelicals, and those deeper roots which have sustained us must be cultivated, appreciated, taught, and built upon."

John Van Engen, professor of history at Notre Dame University, can thank God for the covenant promises, for he understands theology and church history. And so can we—because John Van Engen is back again.

30

Fannie H. Smith,
Court Stenographer

Even today in some of our homes, when you stop for coffee after church, you'll find yourself delegated into one of two conversations, depending on your sex—men smoking in the living room, and women, kids on laps, in the kitchen. It's a legacy from our country backgrounds, from a time when men talked weather and harvest over hot cups of coffee, and women, nibbling on flat sugar cookies, swapped new salad recipes and stories about their children. Two worlds once existed, the barn and the kitchen, the livestock and the children, the Men's Society and the Martha Society—"male and female created he them."

But there are no walls in Fannie Smith's home. Years ago, when Maynard and Fannie designed the spacious two-story house overlooking Crystal Lake in south suburban Minneapolis, they built the kitchen appliances into the outside walls and created a meadow-like living area, thirty feet by thirty. Fannie can't possibly be locked in the kitchen, and women and men would find it next to impossible to segregate themselves, their concerns, or their conversations.

Whether or not it was a strategy of design, the openness of the Smith home typifies the story of Fannie Hannenburg Smith. Born and reared in rural Pease, Minnesota, she moved to Grand Rapids at the age of eighteen, about 1941, like so many others before and after, looking for excitement and change in the only city most CR parents wouldn't consider Babylon. The war was on. Jobs were plentiful. She sewed parachutes seven days a week, eight hours a day, at Hayes Manufacturing in north Grand Rapids. She went to school, night school, where her counselor laughed when she told him she wanted to be a court stenographer. "That's a man's job," he said. His attitude sealed her resolution and made moot the case of Fannie Hannenburg's future.

Two years of parachute seams paid for a move to Chicago and a new start. She lived at the Y. At Gregg College, a stenographic school, a man watched her drag her left hand across the page ahead of her pen when she wrote, and he sent her on her way. But the Stenotype School of Chicago took her, and two years later, the progress of her education having sometimes been hindered by the necessity of outside work, she looked for a job. "Give me a list of the ten best law firms in Chicago," she told them at the school when she graduated, a legal secretary.

She started at the top of the list, one at a time, knocking on doors. She moved down just a few notches before she landed a job with a bigwig named Schuyler—"a Dutchman," she says, "but not much like Christian Reformed"—a close friend of Dwight Eisenhower. She remembers serving Ike lunch, a duty that came with the job, in the law firm's book-lined, regal dining quarters.

It was 1946, and Fannie Hannenburg, country girl, now qualified as a court stenographer, found herself in the middle of the muddle of Chicago party politics, working for a freelance agency that hired out to government bureaus, including the Election Commission. One day a strange man approached her. "Here's fifty dollars," he told her. "Just keep it." When she returned to the office, she told the others that someone had simply come up to her and given her fifty dollars. She heard a roomful of moans and groans.

She says it was very exciting work, but sometimes seamy. "I worked for a judge who had two pairs of glasses," she says, "one for the press—he couldn't even see out of them—and the other for work." She saw him—a symbol of authority and justice—decide cases of voter fraud in the privacy of his chambers before the proceedings, then sit in court, robed in black, and listen to the cases as if he were actually interested in what was transpiring. She laughs now when she remembers. She loved the work, still does.

"Those days in Chicago, if someone would challenge your voting registration with an affidavit, you couldn't vote," she explains. "And it happened all the time to people from Moody Bible Institute. Everybody knew they were Republicans. The challenging affidavits would be signed by the same commissioner who heard Moody's complaints. Judges would try derelicts who were caught voting thirty-five times—more or less— and then give them room and board in the workhouse during the cold winter months."

It was exciting work, sometimes too exciting. Once, in the heat of a divorce hearing, the husband's lawyer accused her of not taking notes. "Read what you've got!" he said. Fannie had missed several minutes of proceedings, overwhelmed by the distraught husband's plea for another chance. "I still love her," he had said, in tears. Fannie Smith had absolutely forgotten who she was.

It was exciting, but she wanted to be closer to her Minnesota home, so she moved to the Minneapolis-St. Paul area and created her own freelance agency in the city, two or three stenographers and several homemakers to type the proceedings at home. "The court was really a man's world," she says. "I was one of only three women stenographers in the state." Called into court one day to replace a man who was ill, she was

Fannie Hannenburg Smith:
living with what she knows.

surprised to hear the judge excuse the jury and pull the lawyers and herself into his chambers, just minutes after she'd arrived. "I can't have a lady in my court," he told them. "What happens if there's foul language used?" She told him she knew how to write and spell as well as anyone, but he said no and recessed the proceeding, hoping the sick man would have a speedy recovery. He must have; she wasn't asked back.

Today she has an officialship, appointed by the judge of Minnesota's first judicial district, which includes much of the Twin Cities metropolitan area. She's been with this judge for fourteen years now, court stenographer, personal secretary, and occasionally something of an advisor—"I let him know how I think at times," she says. And her agenda is a scrapbook of society's ills—murders and other felonies, divorce litigation and civil suits involving millions of dollars, child custody cases. Besides punching out the proceedings on her stenograph and doing secretarial work, Fannie sometimes protects the judge. "There no such thing as a tie in court," she says. "Half the people involved are angry losers. I hear from them later on the phone."

Today, Valentine's Day 1981, she chuckles about it all—the corruption, the discrimination, the parade of very human nature she witnesses and records daily with her fingers and her mind. But it's not a sarcastic laugh, not disillusioned, not pharisaical. The chuckle is the sincere response of a country girl who understands and can live with what she knows. Perhaps it's a laugh of accommodation, the acceptance of humankind's natural condition, our depravity, a genial acceptance of the way things really are. She laughs like Chaucer might have, lovingly.

Fannie Smith is no crusader, despite her scars, because she's not been embittered. She's just Fannie Smith—stenographer, wife, mother—in whatever order. Four generations back, her family lived near La

251

Crosse, Wisconsin, on the banks of the Mississippi. Most every one of them is gone from there now, but all of the children set up housekeeping close to the water. Fannie's house faces the lake with the southern wall of windows. So Crystal Lake is like a family member, even today, its trees stripped by winter, its blue-green breaking surface overlaid by ice and snow. There are fishing shanties out there, and a man on a hang glider being pulled aloft by a truck. It's her backyard. Water is, consciously or unconsciously, part of her heritage.

And so is her church. She's been a member of the Christian Reformed Church her entire life, a significant part of the Twin Cities' churches. "I don't like to criticize the church," she says. "I think we have the closest interpretation of the Bible of any denomination or tradition, and we're very learned in biblical and doctrinal knowledge. But we're weak on evangelism. We know a lot of answers, but we don't *do* enough, and I'm as guilty of that as anyone."

She has a thin face, and a calm and steady way of talking that dissolves pretentions. "But I get to feeling kind of stuffy when I'm in it too much, you know what I mean? I've got a lot of friends outside of the church. I don't know if that's unique or not, or if it's to be held against me. I guess I need them. They help me to enjoy my church, I guess." She laughs.

"A couple of times in our lives we've talked about leaving the church," she says. Twin Cities' congregations have had the problems inherent in many new Christian Reformed churches. "People who move here from small towns like we did are starting a new life. They're often insecure too—that's natural." She looks away, over the lake. "You've really got to have strong leadership then. Sometimes we haven't had it. Sometimes there's been just too much bickering, always bickering, and no spiritual buildup. We've thought about leaving."

Maynard has been working all day—Valentine's Day

The Smiths' new earth home:
designing and building it themselves.

—on the house next door, the new earth home, built into the ground, complete with solar panels and floor-to-ceiling window drapes, thick as theater curtains. It's their latest project, and if you ask for a tour, you'll get a full share of Fannie Smith enthusiasm. They've designed it together, and Maynard and Michael, 24, the younger of their two sons, are building it themselves, nail by nail. Its tall south windows face the lake, of course.

Today is Valentine's Day—velvety hearts full of milk chocolate candy, catchy cards in blushing red, and little naked cherubs with bows and arrows. Tomorrow is the birthday of Susan B. Anthony—suffragettes, marches, women's lib, ERA. It's a strange juxtaposition of images, but maybe it's strange only to those of us who think the days and ideas are somehow incompatible. Today is Saturday, tomorrow is Sunday to Fannie Smith, wife and mother and court stenographer, however you want to say it. Anyway, tonight she and Maynard are going out for dinner together.

31

Pella's Gary Vermeer

"You've got to remember that I'm first of all a farmer," he says, seriously. It's hard to believe him when he sits behind the desk in his office on the second floor of a brand-new corporate office complex, a spacious skylit brick building on the west edge of nineteen acres of Vermeer Manufacturing Company.

But it's clear that Gary Vermeer, chairman of the board, isn't kidding. He fidgets a lot in the swivel chair, and, when he spots a dozen Canada geese soaring over the fertile farmland just outside his window, he drops whatever it is he's thinking of to watch them float on the strength of a brisk southern breeze.

"Farming is my number one occupation," he says again, as if you hadn't heard it. "I farm more now than I ever did. This business is really a sideline." When he says it, there's no cute smile, no deliberate condescension, because what he says is not meant to be a joke. He's a fourth-generation Dutch-American farmer, his great-grandfather, Brandt Vermeer, having come from Gelderland in 1856 and having settled into a farming operation just "east of town," as they say in Pella, just a flat half mile from the new plant.

Gary Vermeer, like his father and grandfather before him, grew up on the black Iowa soil directly east of Pella. The papers for his land show that the original purchaser was none other than the town patriarch, Dominie Henry Scholte, a man Gary Vermeer very much admires for his gumption, intelligence, and foresight. But Scholte was no farmer; Gary Vermeer is.

And it was the farm of his youth that helped create the Vermeer Manufacturing Company in a not altogether unfamiliar American tale of creativity and hard work and good market sense all coming together in a real success story. It's fair to say, however, that financial success sought the Vermeer enterprise in some ways; big money has never been a prime motivation for Gary Vermeer.

It all started during midwestern winters, when the Iowa farmers do chores, repair machinery, and get ugly with cabin fever just thinking about the sweet taste of spring. After graduating from high school, Gary worked on his father's farm, and during the Januarys and Februarys of the mid-to-late 1930s, when there was no money anywhere, Gary and his father rebuilt a chicken coop, put together a stove out of an oil barrel, and started into the honorable farm vocation of tinkering.

Their first project was an elevator; there were elevators to be bought, for sure, but there was no money to buy them. So Gary built one, and when the neighbors saw the Vermeer elevator perform come harvest time, each of them hinted strongly that he would buy one for sure if Gary could come up with a few more during the next winters. And that's how it started.

Along came the war. The Vermeer farm was, by now, no small operation; in fact, after Gary married Matilda Van Gorp and bought into his own place, father and son agreed that they really needed a two-row cornpicker to handle the crops. Farm machinery, like almost everything else in 1941, was rationed, so they took off to Knoxville to ask the ration board. The powers-that-were said yes—but on one condition: they would have to use it in the neighbor's fields too; a rare piece of machinery like that was far too valuable to be locked up in a shed. They agreed; no problem.

But they did have a wagon problem. Even earlier, Gary thought it an unnecessary burden to have to lift up a whole wagon full of crop in order to get the corn to flow into the Vermeer's homemade elevator, so he spent some time in the farm shop and came up with a mechanical wagon hoist, a simple block-and-tackle operation that lifted the whole bed of the wagon off the chassis. Picking corn through January, the Vermeers visited a whole lot of neighboring farmyards, and when the neighbors saw this newfangled wagon, a number of them insisted that they would like such a thing for themselves.

Gary's cousin Ralph told him rather offhandedly that if Gary and his dad ever started a business, he would like to be in on it. The wagon hoists were a popular item; finally, the farm shop was abandoned for a new block building on Pella's west side. Gary laid the block himself, and now there was a name—Vermeer Manufacturing, of course—and a work force of three men.

Meanwhile, there were other problems on the farm. A farmer needs a hammer mill to grind corn or hay or anything, but the hammer mill, like the farm itself, wasn't of much use during the winter. Run with belts like an old thrasher, the hammer mill, once wet or snowy, was next to useless. The Vermeers got to thinking there had to be a better way.

In the winter of '48, Gary borrowed the power take-off from the cornpicker, picked up a couple of V-pulleys from Des Moines, bolted the whole works on the side of the grinder, and presto! he had a mill for all seasons.

They took it up to "Hay Day" in Monticello, Iowa, a farmland event featuring livestock, cotton candy, a little boot-stomping music, and the newest in farm machinery. "You put some wheels under that thing,

Gary Vermeer:
"first of all a farmer."

and you really got something there," some farmer told him, so the next day he found some wheels and an axle and did just that. They pulled it down to the Iowa State Fair.

When Lindsey Brothers of the Twin Cities, distributors of the mechanical wagon hoist, took a look at the new, transportable hammer mill, they suggested an ad in Iowa's most popular agricultural magazine, *Wallace's Farmer*. Now, up until this time, Vermeer Manufacturing had paid rent on a small mailbox in the Pella post office. In a week, they were carrying inquiries out in a bushel basket, and the three of them decided right then and there it would be a good idea to hire a secretary. In the fall of 1949, they picked up 400 orders in one week with absolutely no way to fill them. For years after that they pushed out 100 units a week, trying to catch up with the orders. Vermeer Manufacturing was growing.

The story of the hammer mill is just one of several similar episodes. Gary never liked digging trenches and laying tile on either his father's place or his own—it was awfully hard work. In 1951, he and his friend, Leonard Maasdam, a local man with an inventive mind, came up with a ditchdigger. Today, pipeliners, municipalities, utilities, tiling contractors, and Gary's farmers all buy the Vermeer diggers—little ones pulled by or mounted on tractors, or big ones that chug along on tracks like those of an army tank.

In 1971, one Sunday morning before church, Gary and a friend walked out on the field, the walk something of a tradition with him. The man told him he was going to sell his cows because he was getting sick and tired of putting up hay, the worst job in farming. Gary thought that was a shame, so he spent some time thinking it over. He knew Allis-Chalmers had long ago proved that round bales, left in the field, wouldn't spoil. "I wonder whether we can't make a baler that will bale a ton of hay at once," he told the people in the experimental department. So they hammered together some four-by-eight plywood sheets and tried to guess how big a ton of hay would be. In March 1971 the prototype was hauled out to some diverted acres of broom grass. The thing didn't work; the hay wouldn't turn inside the chamber.

Gary sawed off a hunk of a fence pole from a nearby pile to make it the same length as the chamber and set the pole into the baler. Sure enough, if the hay didn't wind itself around the pole! In 1972, Vermeer built 100 balers; in the years that followed, their production went to 3,000, 6,000, and, in 1977, 10,000. Today the Vermeer baler has changed baling operations throughout the world; today it accounts for half of the company's business. The company itself has grown to some 800 employees.

Not everything worked, of course. A number of brainstorms just didn't operate in the field like they appeared to on paper. Among other failures, Gary spent months on a barn cleaner, an end-gate seeder, and, of all things, a gravedigger. "Worked fine in soft soil," Gary says, "but couldn't do a thing in frost or rock."

Gary Vermeer looks like a farmer. To some that would be no compliment, but to him it is. He is tall and muscular, straight and strong. He's sixty-two years old, but if it weren't for the Vermeer baler, no one would doubt that he could put up hay with the best wrestlers from the local high school.

And he talks like a farmer, in tight, measured sentences that are meant to be exact answers, full and complete. To some, his speech may seem abrupt, maybe "short," as some people say, but it is no affectation of character. To spend an hour with him in his office is to be convinced of his devotion to farming. His physique, his speech, his actions illustrate that Gary Vermeer is much more comfortable on the rumbling seat of a tractor than in the well-padded chair of the company headmaster.

Vermeer baler:
half the business.

But there are differences between Gary Vermeer and thousands of other Christian Reformed farmers, obviously. For one thing, the company has given him many opportunities to travel. He has worshiped in Dutch Reformed churches in South America, South Africa, Australia, and the Netherlands, and the experiences have helped him to understand the Reformed family of churches. He sees them in a perspective few of us are able to visualize.

"I suppose I'm Christian Reformed because I was born in it," he says, "just like 90 percent of us." His great-grandfather was in the Reformed church, and his grandfather purposely joined Pella's Second Reformed Church in the 1890s because that church had English services and Grandpa Vermeer wanted to be an American. Gary never did discover why either of them eventually joined the Christian Reformed Church when Koene Vanden Bosch, visiting Scholte's colony, recommended that some dissenters join up with a new denomination. "It probably was one of them little fights that were always going on," he says, laughing. "I guess you've got to have those little wars in the Dutch Reformed churches. It seems like they have them all over. Once you get away from them, some years pass, they usually seem so little."

He's been an elder, and he says that family visiting has given him great optimism for the future of his denomination. "Sometimes I think our young people are better than the older ones. They are working hard at bringing up strong families, very loyal people. Some of the old ones can only think about how bad things are; they're always dissatisfied with the church."

In mid-April in Pella, gray-haired men in white shirts and suspenders pull dandelions out of the front lawn of Dominie Scholte's big house on the north end of the town square. Soon it will be Tulip Time in Pella, and Gary Vermeer, all decked out in his Gelderland costume, will stand up in Scholte's own library and tell visitors from Des Moines and Dubuque about the dominie, a man he very much admires.

There's a world of difference between them—Scholte, a European aristocrat, a philosopher, a politician, a Darbyite; and Gary Vermeer, an American farmer, a tinkerer, a mechanic, an industrialist. But another century down the road, at this time of the year, likely as not somebody, all decked out in a bib overall, will stand up and tell out-of-towners about Gary Vermeer, the farmer-inventor who made good, and somebody else will be pulling the dandelions from the grass beneath the first Vermeer mechanical wagon hoist.

32

Mary

This scrapbook is a collection of pictures from the life of Mary, one of God's people called Christian Reformed. All the names in this story are fictitious.

1955. She never really had a father. Oh, there was her Uncle Bill, and Grandpa, of course; they were always around the house, but nobody looked at her mom the way this new man did. And her mom never looked at anyone, except her, of course, the way she looked at him all the time. And he kissed her too often, way too often. And he hugged her too. And all the time she had to watch that mushy stuff. And it just wasn't fair at all.

That's why she wanted to run away, to go back to Grandma's house in Chicago.

But her bike lay in the ditch in the weeds, just where she had left it when she decided that she didn't know where Chicago was from Michigan. Her little plaid suitcase had dropped out of the front basket.

And now it was getting late. Late like when she came home from school. Suppertime. That late. And besides, she was getting hungry now. But she wouldn't go back, no sir.

Maybe they'll find me dead here in the ditch, she told herself.

When the car stopped next to her, she pretended to

cry, and when that man, that friend of her mother's, when he sat down in the grass next to her, she pretended she was mad about everything.

"Come home," he said. "I'll take you home."

He was strong. He picked up her whole bike in his hands real easy, like it was just a little toy.

"C'mon," he said, his hand out.

And she knew she had a father.

1964. Grandma knew it, and she knew it too. Long ago, thirty years, maybe, the doctors had told Grandma that her disease would take her home to heaven in five months.

But now, years later, she was dying. It had been almost a year since Mary had graduated from high school and come to stay with Grandma, keeping the house, cleaning, cooking. And now, this Thursday, both of them knew Grandma was dying.

"Sit down," Grandma said. "Sit down here."

Grandma's eyes were clear, but her face was gray and her cheeks, thin and wrinkled, pulled back at the corners of her mouth where little white flecks formed.

"Your mother will never tell you," she said. Then she inhaled. "You should know about your father," she said, "your real father." Her eyes fluttered a bit as she stared at the ceiling. "He would have married your mother, you know. He said he would, but your mother had you all alone. Most of Roseland thought she was wrong. But she had you alone. You respect her, Mary, you respect your mother." She coughed slightly. "I think you should know the whole story. Your mother would never tell you. You respect your mother, Mary."

Grandma died the next day, Good Friday.

1965. She had never imagined it would be like this. Just an old gray house, an official-looking man in a suit and a mustache behind a big, old desk, just herself and her boyfriend and a couple of friends for witnesses. But then she never imagined love could be like this either.

When she looked into his eyes, she saw nothing but happiness, the conviction of love and trust, the firm resolve that all their problems—even her parents' refusal to go along with the marriage—everything could work out with a little love and time and some prayer.

"And you take this man, my dear?" the justice of the peace said.

"Oh, yes," she said.

Was it only two months since that first date? It seemed so long, and when she looked at him—his face, his neck, his shoulders—she wondered how she ever had lived without him, how so much of her life could have already passed. Besides, she knew it was the right thing. In a few months he would be gone—Vietnam? Germany? And she would love him, support him with daily letters, give him what he needed to come home to. It had to be right. She had prayed about it.

1973. It's not that she hadn't thought of the possibility before, especially with his spending close to a hundred a week for beer. There had to be some willing women in those bars. He had to have opportunities, probably lots of them.

So when he admitted it had happened, she had been able to stay strong, to appear tough. She didn't cry because she wanted him to see her toughness.

But the next day, two of the three kids off to school, she cried all day, because she couldn't clean her mind of her own husband, alone, with some other faceless woman. She tried to rinse the picture from her mind, but it stayed right there, all day. She tried to pray it away, but it hung there like a thick curtain. Forgivable, yes, but not forgettable.

"You're just too perfect for me," he had told her. She wondered if it was true, and she wondered if marriage or personal honor was more important. She didn't know what was right. She didn't remember any easy answers from her years at Christian High.

1975. When the phone rang, she was surprised to find that she had even slept. It had been that kind of day. She had found a trailer right away that morning. And the church, her old church, had been so friendly and wonderful on Sunday. Her mother and stepfather were doing all they could, already calling some church friends about a needed appliance or a table. It would be a new chance, a second chance for them.

She realized that she had nearly forgotten the phone. She scrambled downstairs, sure that it was he calling her here in her parents' house. She remembered the smile on his face when he had said, "Okay, let's start all over again." She already had lined up a job, and he could get one easily—he was so handy.

"Your husband is gone, Mary," the voice said. It was his mother; she was crying. "He sold the house like he promised, but he let out for Montana. I can't tell you how badly—"

Towels, a couple of sheets, and some clothes, she thought as she hung up the phone. And three kids with no father. And no husband. And no money. Her mother held her tightly, but said nothing. It was late. Or was it early? She felt alone in her own parents' home—alone and deserted.

1976. They prayed together even though it wasn't suppertime. She interrupted the cartoons and pulled the kids into the kitchen, and she prayed for a job, even though she knew very well there was little chance.

Two whole days she had stood in line at the armory, waiting—not even for a job, but just the opportunity to get an interview. And finally, three chances, only one of which would fit the kids' school schedule.

"We've had sixteen applicants already," the lady had told her, "sixteen well-qualified applicants. I don't want you to get your hopes up. You understand?"

She had no hopes, of course. What was she really? A deserted mother, sole provider for three children, living in other people's rummage. It wasn't hope that

Maybe they'll find me
dead here in the ditch, she told herself.

kept her in line at the armory, amid the guns and the banners and the flags, the symbols of manhood. It wasn't hope because hope belonged to the hopeful. She had stayed because there was nothing else, nowhere else to go.

"We'll call you," the woman had said.

The kids went back into the TV room.

And the phone rang as clearly as a voice from heaven, and all she said was "Yes."

1977. The church softball team went 15-1 that year, and the only game they lost was close. If Henry Aaldersma hadn't been working third shift, they'd have won that one too.

Her kids loved the games. It got them out of the trailer and in with their friends from church. She saw to it that they made it to nearly every game.

"Henry Aaldersma isn't doing anything," Johnny said. "Why don't you ask him over for coffee, Mom?"

She smiled.

"C'mon, Mom, please? We like him. He's really nice, and he's such a dumb good player."

Henry was older than she was, but he was lean and muscular. He looked like a man.

He was divorced. So was she. But he was a man. Underneath everything else, he was a man.

"Not tonight," she told the kids.

"But I asked him. He said he had to work at ten, but he had nothing to do for an hour."

She shook her head and smiled.

"Awww, Mom—"

"Okay, go ask him."

1978. She told herself it was strange how they could spend so much time together. He'd be over two, three times a week—just talking, coffee steaming away in the cup he always held with both hands. Somehow she didn't feel guilty when she talked to him, unlike some of the others from the church. They were the same really—same beliefs, same feelings, and most important, the same experience. They could spend hours with their elbows up on the formica tabletop.

They would walk out to his truck together about ten or so on warm summer nights. But she knew it was getting harder to let him leave.

And she didn't remember what it was exactly they were talking about when he mentioned it, just out of the blue, finally, even though they both had been thinking it for a long time.

"You know," he said, "it's going to be three years before I can marry you." His elbow poked out of the window of the pickup, and there was no particular smile on his face.

In a way it wasn't a shock, and she didn't act surprised. She didn't have to act as if he were popping the question because she wasn't a teenager and neither was he.

But she smiled as he drove off to the third shift because she knew that he had meant it the way he had said, just a kind of fact, something they both would have to deal with. Three years and his oldest boys would be out on their own. Three years, he had said. Three years was still a whole lot of time.

1980. This time it was a church wedding, four grandparents, eight kids, and a church full of people, happy people.

She was sure of things this time. Henry looked handsome and confident. She couldn't help thinking of his problems, of their problems. He had told her long ago about his drinking, but then he had been fired—sleeping on the third shift. But his counselor had said Henry didn't need the group anymore. "He's okay," he had told her over the phone. "Seems as if he doesn't need anybody else's motivation to stop now. He's got his own."

And then there were the kids standing there, all eight of them. Her family now. Her problems too. She remembered her own stepfather picking up her bike along the road.

It went very well that day, very well, and it was the day after Thanksgiving. Another holiday, really. Not just turkey and stuffing either. A real holiday.

But Henry's mother, all dressed up as if it were her first wedding, hugged her afterward, as the organ music still rolled out of the sanctuary. She kissed her too, and she said, "Mary, I want to thank you for marrying my son." And then she quickly pulled away. After all, the greeting line was already forming, and it wouldn't be so good to be standing there with a handkerchief up to your eyes. Not today.

1981. There's a self-portrait of Henry's oldest son, Jeff, in the house. He's a strong-looking kid with long, black curls and a neck as thick as a wrestler's. His eyes are blue and piercing, and he's looking up and out into an almost violent blue background. All the colors are bright and charged, almost visionary.

Jeff spent some time doing portraits at an amusement park, nearly a year. And he's been kicked out of his mother's house, and he's been kicked out of his father's house, and he's left home, lived and worked in Missouri.

Five years ago, when his mother left Henry, she took him to the Baptist church, and for a time he was part of the Pentecostal church not so far away.

But today he's bitter, and Mary knows it because she's seen it in her oldest stepson. He's bitter toward the church, toward his father, toward everyone. He's in Germany now, by himself, in the army.

His self-portrait looks handsome, but proud and defiant. And it stands here as a reminder that prayer is a continuous thing at the Aaldersma home, just one of hundreds like it on the suburban streets of this continent.

Henry and Mary Aaldersma still put their elbows up on the table, and Henry still holds the cup in both hands when he takes a sip. They have each other now because they need each other.

But Jeff's self-portrait reminds them and us that fathers and mothers and love itself and respect and authority and marriage have all been charred by sin. The family requires redemption as fully and earnestly as your soul, or mine.

33

John Norlinger,
Corporate Executive

For some reason, John Norlinger doesn't look like a corporate executive. Maybe it's the sideburns that hide his ears like fine steel wool. Maybe it's the cotton shirt and cardigan sweater where one expect a Hart Schaffner & Marx. Maybe it's his almost boyish sincerity, the blue of his eyes, the roundness of his face, his smile. Not everyone wears a John Norlinger smile; it's a permanent feature of his face, as much a characteristic as his eyebrows.

But he is a corporate executive, vice president of planning and controller at the Electric Display Division of Ball Corporation, a modular brick fortress, surrounded by a chain-link fence and prairie grass and scrub oak groves at the northernmost edge of metropolitan Minneapolis-St. Paul. *Ball* is the name on your grandmother's canning lids, but this division has nothing to do with backyard patches of beets and beans.

John Norlinger's production lines roll out cathode-ray tubes (CRTs in the trade); to the layperson, CRTs are the wide, green screens hanging from airport ceilings—the ones that list arrival and departure times. John Norlinger's division buys steel in coils and sheets, cuts it, shapes it into a chassis, then mounts onto that chassis the video screens it buys from other specialty companies. The division's electronic engineers design intricate circuitry patterns printed on little circuit boards (PCBs) and send them on to assembly, where the maplike outline is "stuffed" with the electronic components the engineers have called for—diodes, transistors, capacitors, resistors—colorful gadgets the size of hairpins. Once "stuffed," tested, and approved, the component board is affixed to the chassis, the screen is fine-tuned, and the completed CRT is boxed and shipped to a customer who specifically ordered the screen to fit his own machine. Taiwan, Korea, Japan, Italy, Spain—John Norlinger's company is multinational in the sense that it depends on offshore suppliers for a significant amount of its parts. Put the whole business together, and the company does business in excess of $30,000,000 annually.

All of fifteen years ago, when transistor radios were only for the rich, when hulking computers took up half an office complex, and when hand-held calculators were beyond anyone's dream, way back then there was no Electronic Display Division of Ball Corporation because there was no electronic computer industry. Today that industry is a reality, and some tell us that the day is not far off when everyone will have a home computer. It's speculation, of course, but there's little else but speculation in the industry. The only sure thing is obsolescence; it lies back there like a continuous counterattack, always threatening. In the electronics industry there's no such thing as tradition, no such thing as a standard product. "A year from now the whole industry may change," John says. "We have to live with that possibility."

And how does that kind of precarious existence affect day-to-day business? Ask John how many units Ball produces annually. "That's classified information," he says, and suddenly the chain-link fence surrounding the place closes in, even though John's own office is spacious and comfortable. *Classified* is a CIA word, but the volatile nature of the electronics industry makes the number of units produced annually a vital statistic for any of the twenty-plus competitors, many of which are foreign, "heavily focused" industries, corporations that have Ball quite high on their own hit lists. "Nobody really knows the size of the market today," he says, the smile still there. "Everybody's got his own guesses, but nobody really knows. Since we're a big part of the market, at least we know what we produce, at least we know something that others don't." He sits in a modern, earth-toned chair, its arms of blond oak, and his hands, fingers together in front of his face as he speaks, point out the significant phrases. But he doesn't look like a cloak-and-dagger man either.

"A few years ago every color TV on the planet was made in this country," he says. "Today they are all foreign-made." It's John Norlinger's job to keep that kind of thing from happening to Ball's CRT production. In addition to its volatile nature, it is an extremely competitive business. "We try to buy domestic materials as a kind of commitment," he says, "but it's a tough industry. Sometimes we are forced to buy from Taiwan or Japan or Korea just to stay in business with them." The names of his competitors are already household words to us—Panasonic, Hitachi—massive corporations that have threatened and even destroyed some domestic companies. John's specific job description is to plan the strategic direction of the company over the next five years, to develop and implement the short-range operating plan. His decisions are central to the viability of the company.

And today, outside the barrier of the chain-link fence, a half-dozen women sit in cars and vans while their strike signs stand in empty boxes like sleeping sentries. A walkout compounds the problems, of course, because higher wages mean higher prices, and higher prices destroy the competitive edge. Higher prices mean fewer jobs. At upwards of $6.00 an hour starting pay for stuffing PCBs—a job that most anyone

John Norlinger:
smiling at twenty-plus competitors.

can learn in a half day—pay seems adequately compensatory when balanced with the very real risk of death in such a volatile industry. That's management's position, of course, but it's just one more reason that John Norlinger shouldn't be wearing his smile.

But it's there nonetheless. Why? One reason is his love for the job, despite its secrecy, its competitiveness, its problems. "I always wanted to be an accountant," he says, "even though I never knew one." Already at eleven years old, John Norlinger, a third-generation Norwegian-American, was keeping the books on his father's dairy near Osakis, Minnesota. After high school he spent four Air Force years on America's first-line bomber, the B-52, as a radar technician, an experience that acquainted him with the most sophisticated electronic gadgetry of the late 50s. After the Air Force, he picked up a degree in accounting from Mankato State University in three and one-half years, while working a fulltime job. Today he is doing what he feels he always wanted to do. Not many of us are so blessed. A sense of calling prompts the smile.

But there's more to it. John is happy with his church. Born and reared as a Lutheran, for a period a Methodist, John Norlinger spotted the Faith Christian Reformed Church of New Brighton one afternoon after moving to the northern suburbs, and he told his wife, Gloria ("she's a Swede—that's the next best thing to a Norwegian"), that they would try it out come next Sunday. They did. John and Gloria and their two boys, Thad and Jay, have been there ever since, over six years.

Somewhat disenchanted with the tradition-bound churches of his past, John appreciates Faith CRC because, as he felt almost immediately, the people there base themselves, their problems, their understanding of the world itself upon the Word alone. "It was a total emphasis," he says, "and we felt it from the first time we went there." It was a year before they joined. "Some of those doctrines—election, for instance —were very hard to swallow for someone who had always distrusted the institutional church. But God's will prevails over man's stubbornness," he says. "I lost my critical fervor against the organized church; it was something I had since I was a kid, and I think it's gone today because I've found that my religion has become part of my life, not just some separate experience. It's been really a great experience, the end of a long search."

John Norlinger is what a college coach would call a "walk-on." He came into a Christian Reformed church from the community; he is someone too many of us would still call an "outsider." But his assessment of us on our 125th birthday is especially important because of who he is. "The strength of the CRC today is its continual struggle with the Word, its reliance upon what God says." He is, of course, smiling. "And I observe it in the way things are done—the body politic of the church, for example. Quotas, budgets. The Word is applied. Prayer is significant; its power isn't doubted. I saw it as a deacon.

"But the weakness of the CRC, as I've been in it, is its inability to grow, to achieve growth; it certainly doesn't have a track record of real growth. That's not all bad, of course, but the church, if it's to serve its mission, is going to have to allow for some more latitude in ideas.

"I've seen situations, for instance, when a passage of Scripture is analyzed in a small discussion group. A strictly Calvinist point of view is given. That kind of locking things up can turn newer members off; your development in faith is a gradual, slow path you move along until you die. The CR people, born and reared in the church, are so much further ahead than others; that's why we're small. There just aren't that many people at that advanced point."

It's warm for February; it's warm for a Minneapolis February. The snow is melting fast, and the parking lot is wet, spotted with puddles. "The message of the CRC is just phenomenal," he says, locking the front door behind him on a workless Saturday morning, "but it's got to be shared. It's a strength and maybe a weakness too. The heritage of the CRC is so solid and so firm; God's got to have a big mission coming up. I just really believe that."

He unlocks the gate of the chain-link fence and waves to the strikers when he leaves, smiling. They return the wave and the smile.

34

Craig B. + Andriette P.

"April is the cruelest month," says Eliot, but not everyone believes him. Take Shakespeare, for example:

> "Proud-pied April dress'd in all his trim
> Hath put a spirit of youth in everything."

That's a little sweeter. Or Hopkins:

> Nothing is so beautiful as spring....
> The glassy peartree leaves and blooms, they brush
> The descending blue; that blue is all in a rush
> With richness.

Winter imprisons the American Plains in a frigid cocoon, and "puddle wonderful" spring, like a covenant promise, releases and quickens, brings robins and winter wheat on the sweet warmth of a southern breeze.

On the Plains there is little to stop the spring winds. They roll down from the mountains and sweep across the broken ground, all the while building momentum. They whistle through groves and around barn corners, and they howl through open windows. Farm folk swap the noise for the welcome taste of warmth.

April—and spring—does wondrous things to midwestern college campuses. It draws bicycles like frost out of cold basements; it turns fur-lined parkas into string bikinis; it transforms the raw-red of winter cheeks into glowing Polynesian tones. Motorcycles buzz through streets; frisbees hover and sail in winds hearty enough to hang kites with ten-foot braided tails.

It must have been a chauvinist who said that spring turns a young man's fancy in a particular direction. Once freed from the bondage of ice, all youth glows with the oldest and holiest of human attractions. "What is all this juice and all this joy?" asks Hopkins. It's just spring, rebirth, a new chance, life beginning, renewing itself all over. It's spring fever—the sweetest virus known to college students.

Andriette Pieron and Craig Boersema are in love this spring on the Great Plains. You can see it in their faces. Cow eyes, some call it, that insatiable gaze lovers wear—"as if increase of appetite has grown by what it fed on," says Hamlet. Soon Craig and Andriette will be married, and in their union is represented the history of a church and the hope for its future.

Years ago, Grandpa Boersema worked in the lumber mills of the Pacific Northwest. He was an unskilled worker, one of thousands of Dutch Reformed people who had come to the new country—the United States —to take unskilled jobs as garbage haulers, factory help, hired hands. He settled in Washington—Oak Harbor—and his son, Craig's father, started working for Sears, a step up, perhaps, from the buzz of the saws and the daily habit of clinging sawdust. Craig was born and reared in Marysville; after graduation from Watson Groen Christian High in Seattle, he worked for three years, most of them at Nord Door, a wooden products company that employs an army of Christian Reformed men and women from the Marysville area.

Ever since he worked parttime on a dairy through high school, he has wanted to farm for a living. Nord

Door, for him, was a means to an end, the place where he could accumulate enough capital to fulfill his own version of the American Dream. First he stacked hemlock and fir doors into six-foot piles, separating the rejects from the saleables. Then came a promotion: he started cutting out the nicks and pitch pockets from the rejects to make smaller-sized door panels. Finally, a grade four bench stocker at better than eight dollars an hour—an agreeable job that gave him more freedom, releasing him from the boring bind of the assembly line. Good pay. Good position. But he saw around him too many people who were cutting lumber, gluing doors, or grading panels simply to earn the money they needed to get what they really wanted out of life. For too many, work was not fulfilling. He felt, like them, no sense of calling, no real belief in his work. He too was working for an investment, but his experience at Nord Door made clear that the investment would be an education, a Christian education. "I guess I just knew that if I were to go to college, it would have to be a Christian college," he says.

He could have gone to community colleges in the Marysville area and kept working at the factory. But he opted to end a chapter of his life at Nord Door, to take something of what he had earned and to enroll at Dordt College. In August 1979, three full years out of high school, he drove over the Rockies and onto the Plains to Iowa, having absolutely no idea what it was he wanted to study, knowing only that he wanted his investment, a college education, to have direction, to be Christian.

Craig Boersema represents the third and fourth generations of Dutch families who came to America prior to the 1890s. His ethnoreligious roots, like so many of ours, are pre-Kuyperian; his ancestors immigrated before the Anti-Revolutionary Party, before the rise of the Free University, before the real effects of the *Doleantie*. His background is *Afscheiding*,

*Craig Boersema and Andriette Pieron:
shocked parents.*

separatist, pietist, a world-and-life vision that insists on the demonstration of salvation by one's restraint—by strict Sabbath observance, by clear rejection of a world which is, of course, of the devil.

Andriette Pieron sits with him on a couch in the dormitory room. And she smiles when she hears his story. She knows that there was a time when she, herself an immigrant, a Dutch-Canadian who remembers sitting on the knee of her grandfather's friend, a man she called Oom Herman—Professor Herman Dooyeweerd—there was a time when she could have felt little but scorn for someone the likes of Craig Boersema, someone so provincial, so narrow, so unbelievably old-fashioned that his vision of Christianity can be studied as history today in the Netherlands. And when Andriette talks, Craig smiles, because he knows that just one incredibly long year ago he never could have guessed there were Christian Reformed people like Andriette, good Christians who believe that women should be elders and deacons, strong Christians whose attitudes toward "worldly ways" don't seem to prompt any guilt, strange Christians always talking about "being Reformed" in politics and art and journalism and about everything else on God's green earth.

Andriette Pieron, granddaughter of the *Doleantie,* immigrated with her father, an orthopedic surgeon, and her mother, an elder in the Gereformeerde Kerken, and her three sisters in 1973. Her father, educated at the Free University, had for a time questioned the socialism in the Netherlands and the lack of opportunities available for both himself as a young doctor and his children. He took his family over for a few years and spent some time studying and working in Manitoba before returning to write his Ph.D. thesis at Leiden. Following the family's return to Holland, they simply assumed that they would continue to stay in the country of their grandparents, the country they called home. Then, Andriette says, the girls started seeing letters from an unbelievably strange place—Saskatchewan—a name that none of them could pronounce.

The girls wanted nothing to do with Canada; Andriette's older sister already had a boyfriend. But their father was sure now that the opportunities for him in a practice would be ever so much greater in Regina. So they came back to Canada, but it wasn't easy—Regina, Saskatchewan, in the 1970s was not Orange City, Iowa, or Grand Rapids, Michigan. They knew no one. It was hot in Regina during the summer of 1973; it was especially uncomfortable for a family who was accustomed to the sights and sounds of Europe, a family who suddenly found themselves residents of a Canadian motel, living out of a bedroom while mother and father scoured the area looking for a place to rent in a city with no rentals.

Two hot weeks later they found a townhouse in a seedy section of the city where the only qualification for renting, it seemed, was that you had hordes of uncontrollable kids. "It was awful," she remembers. "My dad had a job, but we had little money." The family bought a hideaway couch for the downstairs—the living room becoming the master bedroom—and the kids slept upstairs on foam slabs. Her two younger sisters, feeling the stubborn reluctance in their siblings, refused to speak English, innocently holding on to some childlike dream that their civil disobedience would somehow prompt a return to Holland. "*Ik weet niet wat je zegt*" ["I don't know what you're saying."], they would tell their mother when she tried to teach them the new language.

"It was hot, we had nothing to do, we had no friends," she says. "It was a real problem." But a year later, a new house, a new school, her father doing well in a good practice, Canada started looking more and more like home. She went to one high school for four years—the longest she had ever stayed anywhere before.

285

Active in Youth for Christ throughout school, Andriette followed the advice of friends and her own romance with Europe and enrolled in the Torchbearer Bible School in Sweden for a year of Baptist-oriented biblical studies. But, when she returned to Canada, she looked to her own church and tradition for further education. She came to Sioux Center, Iowa, and when she remembered her church in Holland—no Sunday evening services, communion open to kids, dances in the church hall—she found she had journeyed back in time.

Craig and Andriette met while looking over copy for the college newspaper, becoming good friends long before they recognized, at first individually, silently, that their friendship was moving in a different, totally unforeseen direction.

Today, warm spring winds are thawing a college campus. Today, somewhat reluctantly, they are in love. "Neither of us wanted anything to do with the usual scene—college as cupid. We were both determined that our purpose in being here was to get an education—not a spouse." They were, fortunately, half wrong about that. "The only people more shocked than we were about what happened were our parents," they admit.

"Our friends tell us that we're from two different cultures," Craig admits, "but somehow it doesn't seem so strange to us." Their friends are right: Craig, a Yankee, a pietist, the *Afscheiding*; Andriette, a Canadian, an immigrant, a neo-Kuyperian. But ask them about the church, and they admit to similar views—almost.

They are devoted to the church that reared them in such strikingly different ways, and their devotion is based on similar assessments of the church's strengths: creeds, doctrines, the applicability of God's sovereignty, the Christian perspective—what many call the world-and-life view of the Reformed faith. Andriette, who has no small acquaintance with other traditions, admits that "the Reformed perspective on life itself is the best confession I've ever seen."

But they are quick to criticize where they see criticism is warranted. Both admit that they feel commitment means much more than denominational loyalty; both are sure that a dead church is no church at all. They cite lack of openness, mechanical prayer in family and in church, the straightjacket of tradition, inability to change in a new age; they cite these things as our weaknesses, their own weaknesses. "Too often the church barely moves because of futuristic fears," Andriette says. "If we put women in as deacons, then this will happen and that will happen, and finally this will happen. Too often the result is a kind of dead orthodoxy," she says.

They sit together, close. But Craig is a shade less strident, perhaps. "I see her point," he says, "but I know the church is simply not ready for a lot of major changes."

Love, potent as it is, has not, will not erase generations of difference quickly. But then, Shakespeare said, "Love is not love which alters when it alteration finds." They'll learn as much themselves; it's written on their faces.

One spring, the poet William Carlos Williams looked on the roadside grasses beginning to grow, and he wrote,

> . . . the profound change
> has come upon them: rooted they
> grip down and begin to awaken.

What Williams noted in nature, in the change of seasons, is the story of Craig and Andriette, really, on the Plains, this April. And, in them, it's ours too.